Healing Trauma with Magic Mushrooms

A Comprehensive Guide to Microdosing and Macrodosing Psilocybin for PTSD

By True Eira

Ancient Wisdom for Modern Healing

Visit

trueeira.com/test

Find Your Microdose Personality

TRUE
EIRA

ABOUT AUTHOR

Travis Eric, at the helm of True Eira, is a passionate advocate for healing trauma through innovative approaches. As an experienced cultivator of various Psilocybe cubensis strains, he leads a grassroots movement focused on utilizing psilocybin for profound healing journeys and microdosing practices. With a deep commitment to helping others, Travis heads a research team dedicated to staying abreast of the latest scientific literature on psychedelic therapy.

Under his guidance, True Eira has become a beacon for those seeking alternative healing methods. Travis's expertise in mushroom cultivation, combined with his dedication to scientific rigor, positions him uniquely to offer insights into the therapeutic use of psilocybin. "Healing Trauma with Magic Mushrooms" is not just a book but a reflection of Travis's journey and his dedication to aiding others in their healing process. The work encapsulates his extensive knowledge and his heartfelt mission to guide individuals towards overcoming trauma and achieving personal transformation.

TRUE
EIRA

Disclaimer: The information provided in this book is for general informational purposes only. The author makes no representations or warranties of any kind, express or implied, about the completeness, accuracy, reliability, suitability, or availability of the information contained in this book. Any reliance you place on such information is strictly at your own risk.

Table of Contents

True Eira

Ancient Wisdom for Modern Healing

Visit

trueeira.com/test

Find Your Microdose Personality

TRUE
EIRA

Introduction

Welcome to "Healing Trauma with Magic Mushrooms: A Comprehensive Guide to Microdosing and Macrodosing for PTSD." In recent years, we have witnessed a resurgence of interest in the potential of psychedelic substances to address various mental health challenges. Among these challenges, post-traumatic stress disorder (PTSD) stands out as a condition that has proven remarkably resistant to conventional treatments, leaving many searching for alternative solutions. This book is your guide to understanding the transformative potential of magic mushrooms in treating PTSD, focusing on the distinct practices of microdosing and macrodosing.

The following pages will delve into magic mushrooms, their active compound, psilocybin, and how they interact with the brain to create lasting, positive changes. We will explore the impact of PTSD on the mind and body and how these powerful fungi can help facilitate healing, self-discovery, and personal growth. By examining the nuances of microdosing and macrodosing, this book aims to equip you with the knowledge and understanding to tailor your healing journey to your individual needs and experiences.

This guide will cover various topics, including the science behind magic mushrooms, the benefits and risks associated with microdosing and macrodosing, legal and ethical considerations, and the importance of integration and ongoing support. Our goal is to provide you with a comprehensive understanding of the potential of magic mushrooms in transforming lives and to offer practical advice and guidance for those seeking an alternative path to healing PTSD.

As you embark on this journey, we invite you to keep an open mind, approach the information with curiosity, and remember that healing is a personal and unique process. Together, we will explore the potential of magic mushrooms to revolutionize how we approach and treat PTSD and, ultimately, to foster a deeper connection with ourselves and the world around us.

The primary aim of this book is to offer an evidence-based examination of the role of magic mushrooms in treating PTSD. We intend to educate readers on the scientific foundations of PTSD and the use of magic mushrooms for its treatment. Additionally, the book provides practical guidance, covering both the risks and benefits associated with microdosing and macrodosing and ethical considerations. We've also included real-life case studies and testimonials to offer a well-rounded view of this treatment alternative.

This guide is designed for a broad readership. Whether you are an individual suffering from PTSD in search of alternative treatment options, a healthcare provider keen on expanding your therapeutic range, a policy-maker or advocate intrigued by the evolving legal landscape, or a researcher aiming to understand the burgeoning field of psychedelic therapies, there's something here for you.

To maximize the benefits of this comprehensive guide, we recommend reading it in its entirety for a complete understanding. However, the book is structured so each chapter can stand alone, providing valuable insights into specific topics. This allows you to jump to the sections most relevant to your needs, whether you're new to the subject or already have some background.

Overview of PTSD

Post-traumatic stress disorder (PTSD) is a nuanced mental health condition that arises in individuals who have experienced or witnessed a life-altering event. These traumatic incidents can range from natural disasters and accidents to acts of violence, abuse, and warfare. The lingering psychological impact manifests in various symptoms, profoundly disrupting an individual's quality of life.

The symptoms of PTSD are generally categorized into four main areas. First, there are intrusive memories, where recurring, unwelcome, and distressing recollections of the traumatic event plague individuals. These memories, which often spring up without warning, can be triggered by various stimuli reminiscent of the trauma. They may appear as vivid flashbacks, making it feel like the individual relives the trauma, or as nightmares contributing to sleep disturbances.

Secondly, PTSD sufferers frequently exhibit avoidance behaviors. They might deliberately steer clear of people, settings, or situations that evoke memories of the traumatic event. This avoidance can contribute to social isolation and disengagement from activities that were once sources of joy.

The third category involves negative alterations in mood and cognition. Individuals with PTSD may experience persistent negative emotions such as fear, anger, guilt, and shame. These emotional changes often accompany a diminished interest in previously enjoyed activities, a feeling of detachment from others, and difficulties with memory and concentration.

Lastly, heightened arousal and reactivity are common. This manifests as increased irritability, sleep disturbances, hypervigilance, and exaggerated startle responses, all contributing to a chronic state of stress and anxiety.

Given the wide variability in the severity and duration of symptoms among individuals, it's essential to explore diverse treatment options that can be customized to each person's unique needs. This book will introduce you to the promising potential of using magic mushrooms in microdosing and macrodosing formats as alternative approaches for treating and transforming lives affected by PTSD.

To better understand the nuances of PTSD, it's crucial to look at the official definition and diagnostic criteria. According to the Diagnostic and Statistical Manual of Mental Disorders (DSM-5), PTSD is classified based on specific symptoms that arise after exposure to one or more traumatic events. These symptoms must persist for at least one month and cause significant impairment in social, occupational, or other important areas of functioning to meet the diagnosis criteria. It's also worth noting that PTSD can be chronic, lasting for years, or acute, appearing soon after a traumatic event and lasting a shorter period.

Discussing prevalence and demographics, PTSD does not discriminate; it can affect anyone regardless of age, gender, ethnicity, or socioeconomic status. However, specific populations may be at higher risk due to exposure to specific types of trauma. For instance, military veterans, first responders, and survivors of sexual assault frequently report higher incidences of PTSD. Statistics suggest that about 6-8% of the general population will experience PTSD at some point in their lifetime, with rates being somewhat higher among women than men.

As for traditional treatment approaches, options have typically been rooted in psychotherapy and pharmacotherapy. Cognitive Behavioral Therapy (CBT), particularly trauma-focused CBT, and Eye Movement Desensitization and Reprocessing (EMDR) are commonly used psychological treatments. On the pharmacological front, selective serotonin reuptake inhibitors (SSRIs) like sertraline and paroxetine have been approved for treating PTSD. However, these treatments don't work for everyone, and even when effective, they often come with side effects or limitations, highlighting the need for alternative therapies such as magic mushrooms.

By delving into magic mushrooms as an alternative treatment, this book seeks to fill the gaps where traditional approaches may fall short, offering new hope for those grappling with this complex and debilitating condition.

The Potential of Magic Mushrooms for Treating PTSD

Magic mushrooms, scientifically known as psilocybin mushrooms, for treating PTSD has garnered significant attention in recent research. Rich in the psychoactive compound psilocybin, these mushrooms offer therapeutic possibilities through their unique interplay with brain function—most notably in promoting neuroplasticity, enhancing emotional processing, fostering self-awareness, and inducing ego dissolution.

Neuroplasticity refers to the brain's ability to rewire itself, forming new neural connections that allow adaptability and learning. Psilocybin has shown promise in increasing this neuroplasticity, helping individuals with PTSD escape rigid thought cycles and behaviors that aggravate their symptoms. This paves the way for healthier coping mechanisms and fresh perspectives on their experiences.

Psilocybin amplifies emotional processing by strengthening the neural connectivity between critical brain regions, notably the amygdala and the prefrontal cortex. The amygdala plays a crucial role in emotion, particularly fear responses, while the prefrontal cortex governs decision-making, self-awareness, and impulse control. Enhanced communication between these areas can facilitate more effective processing of traumatic memories, decreasing the frequency and severity of nightmares, flashbacks, and other PTSD symptoms.

Magic mushrooms can instigate heightened self-awareness and introspection, enabling individuals to delve deeper into their thoughts, emotions, and experiences. This can lead to critical insights into the root causes and triggers of PTSD, while also aiding in developing more adaptive coping strategies and a nurturing sense of self-compassion.

The ego-dissolving effects of psilocybin can be transformative for those with PTSD. This dissolution of the ego gives rise to a sense of unity and interconnectedness, fostering empathy and a more compassionate understanding of oneself and others. It allows individuals to shed rigid self-concepts and beliefs that their traumatic experiences may have cemented.

The therapeutic properties of magic mushrooms are not a novel discovery; their use dates back centuries across different cultures. Indigenous communities in regions like Central America have used psilocybin mushrooms for spiritual and medicinal purposes. These age-old practices underline the time-tested potential of these fungi to alter human consciousness in beneficial ways. While historical usage was more ceremonial and spiritual, applying these practices to modern-day mental health challenges like PTSD shows promise, drawing a thread from ancient wisdom to contemporary medicine.

Cultural perspectives on the use of magic mushrooms vary widely, reflecting societal attitudes towards psychedelics and mental health treatments. In some cultures, the mushrooms continue to be revered for their spiritual and healing qualities, while in others, they are stigmatized due to legal restrictions and public misconceptions. However, the tides are changing. A renewed interest in psychedelic research is helping to destigmatize these substances and highlight their potential therapeutic value, particularly for conditions as debilitating as PTSD.

Turning to current research and findings, numerous clinical trials and studies have begun to unearth the therapeutic potential of psilocybin in treating PTSD. Recent studies have indicated that psilocybin-assisted therapy can significantly reduce symptoms, improve mental well-being, and enhance the overall quality of life for those affected by PTSD. While research is ongoing, early results are encouraging, showing a solid potential for psilocybin to be an effective treatment modality, often with fewer side effects than traditional methods.

The historical context and the emerging scientific evidence enrich our understanding of the power and potential of magic mushrooms in treating PTSD. As the body of research grows, so does our knowledge, allowing for more targeted and effective treatments: microdosing and macrodosing present distinct but complementary pathways to healing. While microdosing involves ingesting small, sub-perceptual doses that subtly alter mood, cognition, and perception, macrodosing provides a more intense, transformative psychedelic experience. In the subsequent chapters of this book, we will delve deeper into the specific benefits and challenges each approach offers, equipping you with the knowledge to make an informed choice for your healing journey.

Microdosing vs. Macrodosing

In using magic mushrooms for healing and personal growth, it is essential to understand the differences between microdosing and macrodosing, as each approach offers distinct benefits and challenges. Both methods can effectively address PTSD symptoms, but they work uniquely and may be better suited to different individuals or stages of the healing process.

Microdosing: Microdosing involves taking small, sub-perceptual doses of a psychedelic substance, typically between 1/10th and 1/20th of a recreational amount. The goal is to achieve subtle, noticeable mood, cognition, and perception shifts without inducing a full-blown psychedelic experience. Microdosing can offer several benefits for individuals with PTSD, such as:

- Reduced anxiety and depression
- Enhanced creativity and problem-solving abilities
- Improved focus and mental clarity

- Increased empathy and emotional resilience
- Greater openness to new experiences and perspectives

Since microdosing does not produce intense or overwhelming effects, it can be more easily integrated into one's daily life and routine, making it an appealing option for those new to psychedelics or seeking a more gradual and controlled approach to healing.

Macrodosing: Macrodosing, on the other hand, involves taking a larger dose of a psychedelic substance, resulting in a more profound and immersive experience. Macrodosing can provide individuals with PTSD with a transformative and cathartic opportunity to confront and process their trauma, promoting deep emotional healing and self-discovery. Some of the benefits of macrodosing include:

- Enhanced emotional processing and release
- Profound insights into the self and one's trauma
- Ego dissolution and a sense of unity with others
- Heightened self-awareness and self-compassion
- Long-lasting improvements in psychological well-being

While macrodosing can offer powerful therapeutic benefits, it is crucial to consider this approach's potential challenges and risks, such as intense emotional experiences, the potential for a "bad trip," and the need for proper preparation, set and setting, and integration support.

Ultimately, the choice between microdosing and macrodosing depends on the individual's unique needs, preferences, goals, and level of experience and comfort with psychedelics. As we delve deeper into this book, we will explore the nuances of each approach, providing guidance and resources to help you make informed decisions about your healing journey with magic mushrooms and PTSD.

Understanding Magic Mushrooms and PTSD

Before delving into the specifics of microdosing and macrodosing magic mushrooms for PTSD treatment, it is essential to have a solid understanding of the nature of magic mushrooms and the complexities of PTSD. This foundation will provide the context for exploring the potential benefits, risks, and strategies associated with using magic mushrooms to address PTSD symptoms and promote healing.

By understanding the science behind magic mushrooms and the complexities of PTSD, we can better appreciate the potential of psychedelic-assisted therapies and make informed decisions about using microdosing and macrodosing in our healing journeys. This knowledge will serve as a foundation for the book's subsequent sections, where we will explore the practical aspects of using magic mushrooms to address PTSD and promote personal growth.

The Science Behind Magic Mushrooms

Magic mushrooms, also known as psilocybin mushrooms, have been used for centuries in various cultures for spiritual and healing purposes. Modern research sheds light on the science behind these powerful fungi and their potential therapeutic applications. To better understand the potential of magic mushrooms in treating PTSD, it's crucial to examine their essential components and how they interact with our brain and body.

Psilocybin and its effects on the brain: Psilocybin, the key psychoactive component in magic mushrooms, transforms into its active form, psilocin, shortly after ingestion. Psilocin primarily interacts with the brain to produce various mind-altering effects. These effects are mainly achieved through its interaction with specific serotonin receptors in the brain, most notably the 5-HT2A receptor. Engaging with these serotonin receptors can lead to a cascade of neural and psychological changes, resulting in altered states of consciousness ranging from subtle shifts to profound mystical experiences.

Let's start by delving into the biochemistry. Once ingested, the body's enzymes quickly convert psilocybin into psilocin. The latter is a structurally similar compound to serotonin, a neurotransmitter that plays a crucial role in mood regulation, emotional processing, and perception. By binding to serotonin receptors, psilocin disrupts the typical patterns of serotonin transmission. This is thought to lead to increased cross-talk between different brain regions, breaking down the usual barriers between sensory and cognitive areas and producing altered perceptions, thoughts, and emotions.

Regarding microdosing, the psilocin-serotonin interaction is subtle enough to avoid hallucinations but still potent enough to induce noticeable changes in mood, creativity, and mental clarity. Users often report enhanced well-being, increased focus, and heightened emotional sensitivity. These subtle shifts in consciousness can be valuable for those seeking relief from PTSD symptoms, as they may facilitate more adaptive thought patterns and a better emotional equilibrium.

Macrodosing involves taking more significant amounts of psilocybin to induce profound alterations in consciousness, often characterized as mystical or spiritual experiences. Here, the effects on the brain are more pronounced, and users may experience a range of phenomena, including visual and auditory hallucinations, time dilation, ego dissolution, and a deeply felt sense of interconnectedness with all life. These intense experiences can be transformative, particularly for those with PTSD, by providing new perspectives on traumatic events and enabling emotional catharsis. In clinical settings, such incidents have been correlated with long-term improvements in symptoms of depression, anxiety, and indeed PTSD, although more research is needed to understand these outcomes fully.

Psilocybin has been shown to increase neuroplasticity—the brain's ability to form new neural connections. This is particularly important for those with PTSD, as increased neuroplasticity could provide the mental flexibility needed to break free from the ingrained thought patterns and behaviors associated with their trauma.

The effects of psilocybin on the brain are diverse and multi-layered, offering a range of therapeutic opportunities for treating PTSD. From the subtle, mood-enhancing effects of microdosing to the profoundly transformative potential of macrodosing, the psilocybin experience varies in intensity. Still, it holds promise as a unique and powerful tool in mental health.

The role of serotonin and other neurotransmitters: Serotonin, often called the "feel-good" neurotransmitter, is pivotal in shaping our emotional landscape, cognitive functions, and behavior. It regulates various physiological and psychological processes, including mood, appetite, sleep, and social behavior. The relationship between serotonin and mental health conditions like PTSD is complex but critical, especially when considering the therapeutic role of substances like psilocybin mushrooms that directly interact with serotonin receptors in the brain.

When psilocybin is ingested, it is metabolized into psilocin, which has a high affinity for specific serotonin receptors, most notably the 5-HT2A receptor. By binding to these receptors, psilocin can temporarily change the serotonin signaling pathways, leading to psychological effects. This binding doesn't just boost or decrease serotonin levels but modulates the overall balance of neurotransmission in complex ways. It's like introducing a new musician into an orchestra—rather than just increasing the volume, the newcomer changes the whole flow of the music.

For individuals suffering from PTSD, these changes in neurotransmission can be particularly beneficial. Many of the core symptoms of PTSD, such as anxiety, depression, and emotional dysregulation, are linked to imbalances or disruptions in neurotransmitter activity. Specifically, reduced serotonin levels or dysfunctional serotonin receptors have been associated with mood disorders, heightened anxiety, and impaired cognitive function. The modulating effect of psilocin on serotonin receptors can temporarily recalibrate this neurotransmitter imbalance, allowing for a potential respite from these symptoms.

It's not just about serotonin, though. The brain is a complex network, and serotonin interacts with neurotransmitters like dopamine, norepinephrine, and gamma-aminobutyric acid (GABA). Psilocin's effects on serotonin receptors can also indirectly influence these other neurotransmitter systems, adding another layer of complexity to its potential therapeutic effects. For example, dopamine is crucial for motivation and reward processing, and GABA plays a role in calming neural activity and promoting relaxation. Through its action on serotonin receptors, psilocin may be able to indirectly modulate these other neurotransmitters, potentially offering a more holistic approach to treating the multi-faceted symptoms of PTSD.

These neurochemical changes can lay the foundation for more profound psychological shifts. By altering neurotransmitter balance and fostering enhanced neuroplasticity, psilocin may create a favorable environment for cognitive restructuring and emotional processing. This "window of opportunity" could allow individuals to gain new perspectives on their traumatic experiences, assimilate these into a healthier emotional framework, and develop more adaptive coping mechanisms.

The modulation of serotonin and its interplay with other neurotransmitters under the influence of psilocin offers a multi-dimensional approach to alleviating symptoms of PTSD. Whether through microdosing or macrodosing, this serotonin modulation can catalyze broader changes in mood, perception, and thought patterns, offering hope for more effective PTSD treatment options.

Neuroplasticity and the potential for brain rewiring: Neuroplasticity is a groundbreaking concept in neuroscience that has drastically altered our understanding of brain function and adaptability. For many years, scientists believed the brain's structure was relatively fixed and immutable after a certain age. However, current research posits that the brain maintains a lifelong capacity for change and adaptation, even at the cellular level. This is particularly important for individuals with mental health conditions like PTSD, where entrenched neural pathways often contribute to ongoing symptoms.

When discussing neuroplasticity in the context of PTSD and psilocybin treatment, two essential types come to the fore: structural and functional. Structural neuroplasticity refers to the brain's ability to change its physical structure, such as forming new neurons (neurogenesis) or increasing the connections between existing neurons (synaptogenesis). Functional neuroplasticity refers to the brain's ability to reorganize its operational architecture, shifting roles and responsibilities among various neural networks to adapt to new situations, experiences, or in response to damage.

Psilocybin, the psychoactive compound in magic mushrooms, is emerging as a potent facilitator of both types of neuroplasticity. By interacting with specific serotonin receptors in the brain, psilocybin promotes an environment conducive to structural changes, including the growth of new dendrites and synapses. These structural changes can set the stage for functional alterations, enabling the reorganization of neural pathways and thought patterns.

For individuals with PTSD, these changes can be transformative. PTSD symptoms often arise from rigid, maladaptive neural pathways triggered by specific stimuli, leading to flashbacks, nightmares, or extreme emotional states. These pathways can become so well-trodden that they become the brain's default response to certain situations or triggers. Enhanced neuroplasticity could provide the means to "rewire" these deeply ingrained patterns, enabling the formation of new, more adaptive responses to old stimuli. It could allow individuals to overwrite the 'software' of their traumatic memories and emotional responses.

More metaphorically, if your brain's network of neurons were like hiking trails in a forest, PTSD symptoms would be akin to a few overpowering, well-trodden paths that automatically channel all traffic in the exact unhelpful directions. Enhanced neuroplasticity under the influence of psilocybin could be like sending in a team of trailblazers to create new, healthier paths. Over time, as these new routes become more frequently used, the old, unhelpful paths may become overgrown and less dominant, facilitating a more balanced and healthy emotional landscape.

This potential for "brain rewiring" opens up exciting avenues for treatment. With the proper therapeutic guidance, individuals undergoing psilocybin-assisted treatment could learn to capitalize on these periods of heightened neuroplasticity to consciously establish healthier thought patterns, emotional responses, and coping mechanisms, thereby transforming their relationship with their past trauma and potentially achieving lasting healing.

The impact on emotional processing and self-awareness: The realm of emotional processing and self-awareness is a crucial frontier for understanding and treating Post-Traumatic Stress Disorder (PTSD). Emotional processing is not merely the experience of emotion but rather the efficient organization and interpretation of those emotions, integrating them into a coherent emotional response and narrative. On the other hand, self-awareness is a higher cognitive function that allows individuals to understand their internal states, preferences, resources, and intuitions. Both are areas where individuals with PTSD can struggle, but they are also areas where psilocybin therapy shows significant promise.

The psychoactive compound in magic mushrooms, psilocybin, has an uncanny ability to catalyze deep emotional processing. The molecule works partly by enhancing connectivity between different brain regions, notably the amygdala, which plays a crucial role in processing emotions, and the prefrontal cortex, known for its involvement in higher-level thinking, self-awareness, and decision-making. This increased connectivity allows for a more nuanced dialogue between emotional and rational parts of the brain, which can help individuals better process traumatic memories or experiences. In simpler terms, it's as if psilocybin helps 'unstuck' emotions tied to trauma, allowing them to flow and be metabolized by the cognitive brain for a more adaptive understanding and integration.

Alongside enhanced emotional processing, magic mushrooms often induce profound experiences of self-awareness and introspection. Within the safe container of a well-prepared and carefully guided psilocybin session, individuals can frequently investigate their internal world with an unusual level of detachment and curiosity. This is partly due to the phenomenon of 'ego dissolution,' a state where one's usual sense of self softens or even dissolves, allowing for a fresh perspective on ingrained beliefs, patterns, and traumas. In this ego-dissolved state, many report feeling a deep sense of unity and interconnectedness, which can be highly therapeutic for those trapped in the isolating experience of PTSD.

For a person with PTSD, this temporary softening or dissolution of the ego can provide the distance needed to approach traumatic memories and intense emotions without being overwhelmed. In the best scenarios, the individual can revisit these challenging experiences, not as re-traumatizing flashbacks, but as memories that can be viewed from new angles, re-contextualized, and integrated into a broader emotional and cognitive framework. This process can lend itself to developing new coping mechanisms, a more robust sense of self, and even the reframing of the trauma narrative itself. In other words, it allows for a narrative shift from victim to survivor, or even to thriver.

The impacts of such emotional processing and increased self-awareness can be long-lasting and manifest in various ways. They can lead to excellent emotional stability, reduced trigger responses, better interpersonal relationships, and an increased capacity for joy and fulfillment. It's like a psychological 'reset,' offering the possibility of realigning oneself more closely with one's values, desires, and purpose. Of course, the results can vary, and ongoing support—be it through therapy, community, or personal practices—is often needed to integrate these experiences fully. However, the potential for transformative change is significant and places psilocybin as a promising candidate for the future of PTSD treatment.

As we unravel the science behind magic mushrooms, their potential applications in mental health treatment, including for individuals with PTSD, become increasingly apparent. By understanding how these powerful fungi interact with our brain and body, we can better appreciate their potential role in promoting healing and personal growth.

The Complexity of PTSD

Post-traumatic stress disorder (PTSD) is not a one-size-fits-all condition. Its complexities extend far beyond the immediate symptoms, embedding themselves into the very fabric of an individual's life. Understanding these complexities is critical when exploring innovative treatments like magic mushrooms.

Varied Manifestations and Individual Responses: One of the most challenging aspects of treating PTSD is its inherently individualistic nature. A multitude of factors influence how PTSD manifests in different people, and these can range from genetics to early life experiences and even cultural background. Understanding the genetic predisposition of some individuals to PTSD opens a Pandora's box of complicated questions around nature versus nurture. Numerous studies suggest that specific genetic markers might make individuals more susceptible to severe stress responses. These heightened responses can directly influence the experience of trauma, shaping the severity and duration of PTSD symptoms.

Early life experiences add another layer of complexity to the picture. Childhood trauma, neglect, or lack of emotional support can set a person up for a specific reaction to trauma later in life. These early experiences often shape coping mechanisms and stress responses that are deeply ingrained, adding a layer of complexity to PTSD symptoms. Moreover, some individuals with childhood trauma may develop complex PTSD, a subtype of PTSD characterized by emotional dysregulation and severe functional impairment, among other symptoms. Understanding how to navigate this subtype remains an evolving field within psychology.

Another element to consider is one's cultural background. Across the world, societal attitudes toward trauma, mental health, and emotional well-being vary greatly. In some cultures, discussing mental health issues may be taboo, further complicating the recognition and treatment of PTSD symptoms. For example, someone from a culture stigmatizing mental health may be less likely to seek help, making symptom management and recovery all the more difficult. These cultural attitudes can also influence the expression of symptoms. In some societies, emotional or expressive symptoms may be more socially acceptable, while somatic or physical symptoms might be more prevalent in others.

Given these variations, it's no surprise that PTSD does not manifest uniformly across all individuals. Some might primarily suffer from vivid flashbacks and crippling intrusive thoughts, distinguishing past traumas from present reality challenging. Others may experience hyperarousal, perpetually on guard, plagued by insomnia, irritability, and a heightened startle response. This lack of uniformity in symptom expression makes the treatment of PTSD a highly specialized endeavor, requiring a comprehensive, individualized approach.

The individualized nature of PTSD, influenced by genetic factors, early life experiences, and cultural context, makes it a highly complex condition to treat. Personalized treatment plans, therefore, are not just preferable but often necessary. Acknowledging this complexity is the first step in developing more effective, personalized therapeutic strategies for those with PTSD.

Stigma and Societal Understanding: Exploring the societal stigma surrounding PTSD offers a window into the challenges facing those with this condition. Stigma in the context of PTSD often goes beyond the simple misunderstandings or misconceptions about the disorder. It seeps into the cultural fabric insidiously, coloring public opinion and influencing policy. One prevalent misconception is that PTSD primarily affects military veterans or victims of extreme violence, a stereotype that narrowly defines who is "allowed" to have PTSD. This stereotype not only invalidates the experiences of those who've developed PTSD from other forms of trauma but also adds to the societal pressure to "get over it," thereby exacerbating the emotional toll on the affected individuals.

Another aspect of stigma is the stereotyping of symptoms. Many people have a limited understanding of what PTSD looks like and may associate it solely with overtly visible signs of distress, such as hypervigilance or flashbacks. Less understood are the internal struggles like emotional numbness, avoidance, and dissociation, which can be equally debilitating but less "visible." This narrow understanding can lead to a lack of empathy and invalidate the experiences of those whose symptoms manifest less conspicuously.

Stigma also impacts the treatment journey for many individuals with PTSD. Concerns about judgment from family, friends, or employers may make people reluctant to seek diagnosis or treatment. Many fear admitting a mental health disorder like PTSD might affect their employment, relationships, or social standing. This can be especially prevalent in specific professional settings, such as the military or first-responder services, where mental toughness is highly prized. This perception often delays necessary therapeutic intervention, contributing to a deterioration in quality of life over time.

Importantly, stigma doesn't merely originate from the society at large; it can also be internalized by those suffering from PTSD. This self-stigmatization can impact self-esteem and self-worth, making the individual even less likely to seek help. Internalizing society's negative views can compound feelings of isolation, making the road to recovery much more difficult.

As societal understanding of PTSD grows, through academic research and personal narratives, the hope is that these stigmas will diminish. Breaking down these societal barriers is vital not just for the effective treatment of PTSD, but also for the well-being and social inclusion of those affected. Acknowledging the profound impact of stigma on the experience of PTSD underscores the need for multi-dimensional treatment approaches that include societal education and advocacy alongside clinical intervention.

Multi-Dimensional Impact: The multi-dimensional impact of PTSD extends beyond its classification as a mental health disorder, touching upon various aspects of an individual's life. Physical health often deteriorates as stress and hyperarousal symptoms lead to chronic pain, hypertension, and sleep disorders. The body's regular release of stress hormones like cortisol can contribute to long-term health issues, including an increased risk for heart disease and diabetes. This physical toll can worsen psychological symptoms, creating a vicious cycle of declining mental and physical well-being.

Interpersonal relationships also bear the brunt of this condition. The symptoms of PTSD often include emotional withdrawal and avoidance behaviors, putting strain on family bonds and friendships. Emotional numbness may lead to detachment, hindering the individual's ability to engage in meaningful emotional connections. As a result, loved ones may feel helpless, further straining relationships and ending long-standing friendships and partnerships.

Work-life frequently suffers as well. Symptoms such as difficulty focusing and increased irritability can lead to inconsistent work performance. This instability affects financial security and an individual's self-worth and identity. In extreme cases, job loss may occur, adding financial stress to an overwhelming emotional burden. For professionals like military personnel or first responders, who often confront high-stress situations, the stigma surrounding PTSD can make them hesitant to seek help, affecting job performance and career growth.

Psychological symptoms also contribute to a fractured sense of self. Experiencing traumatic events can shatter previous perceptions of the world as safe or just, leading to a reevaluation of one's own identity and place in society. This existential crisis can manifest in harmful coping mechanisms like substance abuse, further complicating the path to recovery.

Given this multi-faceted impact, treating PTSD requires a comprehensive, multi-disciplinary approach. Treatment plans must encompass the psychological, physical, relational, and existential challenges associated with the disorder. By doing so, a more complete path to healing can be offered, tailored to the unique complexities each individual with PTSD faces.

The Limits of Traditional Treatment: Traditional treatment modalities for PTSD, such as psychotherapy and medication, have proven beneficial for many individuals, but they are not without their shortcomings. For instance, pharmaceutical interventions often come with various side effects ranging from mild to severe. Antidepressants may cause fatigue, weight gain, and sexual dysfunction, while anti-anxiety medications can lead to dependency issues. Some patients also report feeling emotionally "numb" when using medication, which can hinder the deeper emotional processing necessary for full recovery. Furthermore, the effectiveness of medication can decrease over time, requiring dosage adjustments and sometimes leading to medication-resistant symptoms.

Psychotherapy, another cornerstone of traditional treatment, comes with its own set of challenges. Although therapeutic interventions like cognitive-behavioral therapy (CBT) and Eye Movement Desensitization and Reprocessing (EMDR) have shown efficacy in treating PTSD, they demand a significant time commitment. Weekly sessions over several months—or even years—can be mentally and emotionally draining. Additionally, not everyone has access to high-quality mental health services. Financial constraints can be a significant barrier, as not all insurance plans cover mental health adequately. Geography also plays a role; those who live in rural areas may find it challenging to access specialized care.

Even when therapy is accessible, cultural factors can impede its effectiveness. For example, veterans or first responders may experience a culture of stoicism and silence surrounding mental health, making it difficult to open up in a therapeutic setting. The stigma around mental health issues can also be more substantial in specific communities, affecting the likelihood that individuals will seek out therapy in the first place.

Both medication and psychotherapy generally aim to treat the symptoms of PTSD rather than its underlying causes. As a result, these treatments sometimes offer only partial relief, leaving unresolved emotional and psychological issues that can resurface later. This is especially concerning given the complex, multi-dimensional nature of PTSD, which often involves not just mental health symptoms but also physical ailments, interpersonal issues, and disruptions to work and daily life.

In light of these limitations, there is a growing interest in complementary and alternative treatments for PTSD, including mindfulness techniques, exercise programs, and emerging therapies like psilocybin. These options aim to address some of the gaps left by traditional therapies, offering a more holistic approach to healing. Understanding the limitations of standard treatment methods provides a more comprehensive picture of the challenges faced by those living with PTSD, and can guide future research and treatment innovation.

Coping Mechanisms and Resilience: Resilience and coping mechanisms hold a significant yet frequently underestimated role in the experience and treatment of PTSD. These inner resources help individuals manage their disorder's symptoms and serve as critical long-term recovery and healing tools. Resiliency and coping mechanisms are not universally consistent; they vary dramatically from person to person, shaped by many factors, including personality traits, past experiences, and cultural background.

For some individuals, social support stands as a crucial coping mechanism. The presence of understanding family members, friends, or support groups can offer an immediate and accessible resource for emotional relief. Sharing experiences and feelings with people who understand can reduce the sense of isolation that often accompanies PTSD. But even the realm of social support is complex; for instance, while some may benefit from a structured setting like group therapy, others might find informal interactions more comforting.

Solitude can also serve as a sanctuary for some. Walking in nature, meditation, or simply contemplating alone can offer the mental space to process traumatic experiences. Here, solitude serves not as isolation but as a form of self-care, offering an environment where the mind can relax and regroup without external pressures.

Creative outlets such as writing, painting, or cooking offer another coping mechanism. They not only serve as a distraction from distressing thoughts but can also act as a form of self-expression, enabling individuals to articulate and externalize their experiences and emotions in a safe, non-judgmental space. The act of creation can become a transformative experience, converting emotional pain into something tangible, perhaps even beautiful, thereby facilitating a unique form of healing.

Physical activity is yet another pathway to resilience. Exercise releases endorphins, naturally elevating mood and offering a healthy, constructive outlet for releasing pent-up emotional and physical tension. Whether through rigorous sports, yoga, or simply regular walks, physical movement can offer immediate and lasting benefits.

Adaptive coping mechanisms like these also contribute to building resilience—the ability to bounce back from adversity. Resilience isn't a static trait but a dynamic quality that can be nurtured and developed. Cognitive techniques for building resilience may include learning to reframe negative thoughts, practicing mindfulness to stay present, and setting achievable goals to rebuild a sense of agency and competence.

Understanding the diverse range of coping mechanisms and the vital role of resilience adds another layer of complexity to treating PTSD. Given this variability, it becomes evident that a one-size-fits-all approach to treatment is inadequate. Treatment plans must be individually tailored, considering each person's unique coping skills and resilience factors. This is essential for developing effective and sustainable therapeutic strategies that empower individuals to participate in their recovery journey actively.

Grasping the complexity of PTSD sets the stage for evaluating the role that innovative therapies, such as magic mushrooms, could play within a broader therapeutic context. With a nuanced appreciation of the condition's many facets, we are better equipped to design more personalized and adaptable treatment plans. These plans may incorporate established methods and alternative therapies, opening the door to using both microdosing and macrodosing with psilocybin mushrooms as potential avenues for healing.

Types of PTSD

When we think of Post-Traumatic Stress Disorder (PTSD), it's crucial to recognize that it isn't a singular, monolithic condition. Instead, PTSD can manifest in various forms, shaped by factors such as the duration of symptoms, the nature of the traumatic event(s), and the time elapsed between the traumatic event and the onset of symptoms. Here, we will explore four commonly recognized types of PTSD: Chronic, Acute, Delayed Onset, and Complex PTSD.

Chronic PTSD: Chronic PTSD, also known as "classic" PTSD, is diagnosed when an individual experiences symptoms for longer than three months. Symptoms can persist for years, sometimes even decades if left untreated. These symptoms may fluctuate in intensity over time but remain a consistent part of the individual's life.

Acute PTSD: Acute PTSD is a short-term form of the disorder where symptoms develop shortly after experiencing a traumatic event and last for less than three months. Even though it's a shorter duration, the impact can still be severe and disruptive. With early and effective treatment, acute PTSD can often be resolved, but if left untreated, it can potentially develop into chronic PTSD.

Delayed-Onset PTSD: In cases of Delayed-Onset PTSD, symptoms may not manifest until six months or more after the traumatic event. This delay can sometimes extend to years, leading to challenges in identifying the connection between the symptoms and the original trauma. People with delayed-onset PTSD may initially present fewer symptoms or might have successfully suppressed or avoided their symptoms until they become too overwhelming to ignore.

Complex PTSD (C-PTSD): Complex PTSD is a form of PTSD that results from prolonged, repeated exposure to traumatic events, often occurring in childhood or adolescence. This can include extended incidents of physical or sexual abuse, long-term domestic violence, or living in a war zone. Individuals with C-PTSD often struggle with additional issues such as difficulties regulating emotions, distorted perceptions of the perpetrator of the abuse, feelings of hopelessness, and interpersonal problems.

Each type of PTSD presents its own unique challenges and may require tailored treatment approaches. Recognizing these different forms of PTSD can allow for more accurate diagnosis, better-targeted treatment, and a more nuanced understanding of the individual experiences of those living with PTSD.

How Trauma Affects the Brain and Body

Trauma affects the individual's immediate response to a threatening situation and can have lasting consequences on their mental and physical health. The impact of trauma on the brain and body is complex and multifaceted, as it can alter how an individual processes and responds to stress, fear, and emotional experiences.

When a person experiences trauma, the amygdala, an area of the brain responsible for processing emotions and encoding memories, becomes highly activated. This heightened activation can form vivid and emotionally charged memories, which can contribute to the development of post-traumatic stress disorder (PTSD) or other trauma-related disorders. Moreover, the hippocampus, a brain region involved in learning and memory, can be negatively affected by excessive stress hormones, potentially impairing its ability to consolidate and retrieve memories correctly.

Another significant consequence of trauma is the dysregulation of the body's stress response system, known as the hypothalamic-pituitary-adrenal (HPA) axis. Prolonged exposure to stress hormones can make the HPA axis less sensitive to feedback signals, making it more challenging for the body to return to a state of balance after a stressful event. This dysregulation can contribute to chronic stress, anxiety, depression, and other mental health issues.

Trauma can also impact the prefrontal cortex, the brain area responsible for executive functions such as decision-making, planning, and impulse control. Chronic stress and trauma can impair the functioning of the prefrontal cortex, which may lead to difficulties in regulating emotions, making decisions, and controlling impulses. These impairments can further exacerbate mental health issues and contribute to maladaptive coping strategies.

In addition to the neurological effects, trauma can manifest physically in the body. Somatic symptoms, such as chronic pain, tension, and gastrointestinal issues, can result from the body's ongoing stress response. Furthermore, trauma can change an individual's posture, movement, and body language as the body unconsciously adopts protective and defensive positions.

Understanding the complex interplay between trauma, the brain, and the body is crucial for developing effective interventions and treatments that address the holistic needs of trauma survivors. Approaches incorporating psychological and somatic components, such as trauma-informed therapy, mindfulness practices, and body-oriented therapies, can be especially beneficial for supporting individuals in their healing journey.

The complex interplay between the amygdala and the prefrontal cortex following trauma can significantly impact an individual's emotional and cognitive functioning. When trauma leads to hyperactivity in the amygdala, the brain's fear and anxiety responses become heightened, which can result in an increased sensitivity to potential threats or triggers in the environment. This heightened sensitivity can make it challenging for the individual to feel safe and at ease, leading to persistent fear, anxiety, and hypervigilance.

At the same time, trauma can dampen the prefrontal cortex, impairing its ability to regulate emotions effectively and manage impulsive behaviors. This impairment can lead to difficulty handling strong emotions, such as anger or sadness. It may result in maladaptive coping strategies, such as substance abuse, self-harm, or other risky behaviors. Furthermore, the reduced functioning of the prefrontal cortex can impact an individual's capacity for decision-making, planning, and problem-solving, making it harder for them to navigate the complexities of daily life.

The amygdala and prefrontal cortex interaction is critical for maintaining emotional balance and resilience. When trauma disrupts this delicate balance, individuals may experience challenges in various aspects of their lives, such as relationships, work, or personal well-being. It is vital for trauma-informed treatment approaches to address these neural imbalances and help restore the optimal functioning of both the amygdala and the prefrontal cortex.

Therapeutic interventions that promote emotional regulation, cognitive restructuring, and the development of adaptive coping skills can be particularly beneficial in this context. Techniques such as cognitive-behavioral therapy, dialectical behavior therapy, and mindfulness-based approaches can help individuals reestablish a healthier balance between the amygdala and the prefrontal cortex, facilitating emotional healing and the development of greater resilience in the face of stress and adversity.

The connection between the brain and body is essential to consider when addressing the impact of trauma on an individual's overall well-being. The nervous system, specifically the autonomic nervous system (ANS), regulates the body's stress response. The ANS has two branches: the sympathetic nervous system (SNS), responsible for the "fight or flight" response, and the parasympathetic nervous system (PNS), responsible for the "rest and digest" response. When trauma disrupts the balance between these two branches, it can have lasting consequences on a person's physical and emotional health.

For individuals who have experienced trauma, the SNS may remain overactivated, keeping the body in constant stress and arousal. This chronic activation can lead to various symptoms, including fatigue, immune system dysregulation, and hormonal imbalances. Furthermore, the continuous stress may make it difficult for the body to transition into a more relaxed, refreshing mode, which is crucial for healing and recovery.

In the context of using entheogens such as magic mushrooms for treating PTSD and trauma-related symptoms, it is essential to recognize their potential to impact the nervous system and restore balance between the SNS and PNS. Psilocybin, the active compound in magic mushrooms, has been shown to influence serotonin receptors in the brain, which can help modulate mood, anxiety, and stress response. This modulation may reduce the overactivation of the SNS, allowing the body to enter a more relaxed state, which is essential for healing and recovery.

Entheogens can also promote experiences of introspection, self-awareness, and emotional processing, which may help individuals confront and process the underlying psychological aspects of their trauma. By addressing trauma's physiological and psychological components, entheogens may offer a comprehensive approach to healing that considers the intricate interplay between the brain and body in trauma recovery.

The Effects of Magic Mushrooms on PTSD Symptoms

Magic mushrooms, containing the psychoactive compound psilocybin, have shown promise as a potential treatment for PTSD due to their unique effects on the brain and the resulting psychological experiences. While research in this area is still emerging, preliminary studies and anecdotal evidence suggest that magic mushrooms can have a significant impact on reducing PTSD symptoms and improving overall well-being.

Psilocybin in magic mushrooms shows promise in supporting emotional healing and cognitive adaptability for those with PTSD. This substance can help individuals process traumatic memories and construct healthier thought patterns by aiding the brain's ability to form new neural connections. These shifts often lead to tangible improvements in various aspects of life, from emotional well-being to daily functionality.

The psychological effects of magic mushrooms can facilitate profound shifts in perception and self-awareness, which can be incredibly beneficial for individuals with PTSD. These shifts can lead to breakthrough moments of clarity, enabling individuals to re-evaluate the meaning and impact of their traumatic experiences on their lives.

Magic mushroom experiences can also foster a sense of connectedness and unity, helping individuals with PTSD feel less isolated and alone in their suffering. By promoting feelings of interconnectedness, these experiences can help to rebuild a sense of trust and safety in the world and in relationships with others, which are often compromised in the aftermath of trauma.

The introspective nature of magic mushroom experiences encourages individuals to explore their internal emotional landscape with more significant curiosity and openness. This exploration can lead to identifying and understanding previously unrecognized patterns of thought, emotion, and behavior, providing individuals with valuable insights into the underlying dynamics contributing to their PTSD symptoms.

Magic mushrooms have been known to facilitate experiences of self-compassion and self-forgiveness. These qualities can be essential in the healing process, as they enable individuals with PTSD to let go of self-blame and shame surrounding their trauma. By fostering a more compassionate and understanding relationship with themselves, individuals can develop a greater sense of inner resilience and the capacity to cope with the challenges that arise from their PTSD.

Addressing the neurological underpinnings of the disorder as well as the emotional, relational, and existential dimensions that contribute to the overall experience of trauma and its aftermath, the psychological effects of magic mushrooms provide a multifaceted approach to healing for individuals with PTSD.

Finally, magic mushrooms have been shown to enhance feelings of connection and empathy for oneself and others. This increased sense of connection can help individuals with PTSD rebuild trust and form healthy relationships, essential components of the healing process. By fostering a sense of belonging and interpersonal support, magic mushrooms may contribute to a more holistic approach to treating PTSD, addressing the condition's neurological, emotional, and social components.

How Magic Mushrooms Impact the Brain and Its Connection to PTSD

Magic mushrooms contain the psychoactive compound psilocybin, which profoundly affects the brain and its functioning. When ingested, psilocybin is converted into psilocin, resembling the neurotransmitter serotonin. Psilocin binds to serotonin receptors in the brain, particularly the 5-HT2A receptor, resulting in a cascade of neurochemical and psychological effects.

The deactivation of the Default Mode Network (DMN) by magic mushrooms is a unique aspect of its potential in treating PTSD. The DMN is often linked with self-referential thoughts and mind-wandering, standard features of PTSD symptoms like rumination and flashbacks. When magic mushrooms disrupt the DMN, they allow for a more fluid state of consciousness, opening the mind to new ways of thinking and feeling. This can lead to profound shifts in how individuals perceive and interpret their traumatic experiences. In this flexible mental state, a person might find it easier to break free from the recurrent, distressing thoughts and feelings that characterize their PTSD.

The temporary dissolution of the DMN creates a therapeutic window for more adaptive and constructive emotional processing, offering a unique avenue for treatment distinct from traditional approaches. This altered state enables individuals to gain fresh perspectives on their trauma and feelings, possibly breaking free from habitual thought patterns. The decrease in DMN activity also fosters a greater emotional connection with oneself and others, crucial for healing and rebuilding social bonds.

The therapeutic window provided by magic mushrooms may also facilitate a deeper connection with one's values, passions, and a sense of purpose in life. This renewed sense of meaning can serve as a powerful motivator for change, inspiring individuals with PTSD to engage more fully in their healing journey and remain committed to recovery.

The magic mushroom experience and its effect on the DMN can be a transformative and healing experience for individuals with PTSD. The increased brain connectivity, novel perspectives, and emotional breakthroughs it facilitates can offer new opportunities for personal growth, emotional healing, and healthier coping mechanisms, ultimately improving overall well-being and quality of life.

Alleviating Specific PTSD Symptoms

Magic mushrooms have the potential to alleviate a wide range of PTSD symptoms, helping individuals regain a sense of control and well-being in their lives. Here, we explore some of the specific ways that magic mushrooms can address common PTSD symptoms:

Intrusive thoughts and flashbacks: Psilocybin's ability to promote neuroplasticity and disrupt the default mode network can help individuals with PTSD process and reframe traumatic memories. This may reduce the frequency and intensity of intrusive thoughts and flashbacks, as the brain learns to integrate these experiences in a healthier manner.

Emotional numbing and detachment: Magic mushrooms can help individuals access and process emotions that may have been suppressed due to trauma. By enhancing emotional awareness and connectivity, psilocybin may enable individuals to reconnect with their feelings and form deeper bonds with others, reducing the sense of emotional numbing and detachment that often accompanies PTSD.

Anxiety and hypervigilance: The psychedelic experience can facilitate a shift in perspective and awareness, allowing individuals with PTSD to view their anxieties differently. This can help break the cycle of hypervigilance and chronic stress by fostering a sense of inner calm and acceptance.

Sleep disturbances and nightmares: Magic mushrooms have been reported to improve sleep quality and reduce the frequency of nightmares in some individuals with PTSD. This may be attributed to the overall reduction in anxiety and the processing of traumatic memories, which can help create a more restful and peaceful state of mind.

Depression and hopelessness: Psilocybin has demonstrated antidepressant effects, which can be particularly beneficial for individuals with PTSD who often experience co-occurring depressive symptoms. By promoting a sense of connection, self-compassion, and meaning, magic mushrooms may help to alleviate feelings of hopelessness and despair.

Avoidance Behavior: Psilocybin has been reported to help individuals face their fears and traumas, possibly leading to decreased avoidance behaviors commonly seen in PTSD. The enhanced emotional and cognitive insight from psilocybin sessions might help sufferers confront and change their avoidance patterns.

Anger and Irritability: Individuals with PTSD often experience heightened irritability and anger. Psilocybin's capacity to induce a sense of interconnectedness and empathy could alleviate these symptoms, helping individuals manage their anger more effectively.

It is important to note that while magic mushrooms may offer relief from specific PTSD symptoms, they are not a one-size-fits-all solution. Each individual's experience will be unique, and the efficacy of magic mushrooms in treating PTSD will depend on factors such as the individual's personal history, the severity of their symptoms, and the support and integration practices available to them.

Efficacy of Psilocybin vs. Traditional Treatments for PTSD

While traditional treatments like Cognitive Behavioral Therapy (CBT) and pharmacotherapy using Selective Serotonin Reuptake Inhibitors (SSRIs) have shown varying degrees of success, psilocybin-assisted therapy is emerging as a novel alternative for treating PTSD. In this section, we will compare the effectiveness of magic mushrooms to these established treatment methods.

Cognitive Behavioral Therapy (CBT)

CBT focuses on identifying and challenging distorted thought patterns and beliefs, helping individuals with PTSD develop more adaptive thoughts and behaviors. While effective for some, CBT can be lengthy and may not provide immediate relief from acute symptoms. Furthermore, CBT primarily focuses on cognitive restructuring and may not adequately address trauma's emotional and existential dimensions.

Selective Serotonin Reuptake Inhibitors (SSRIs)

SSRIs like fluoxetine and sertraline are commonly prescribed for managing PTSD symptoms. These medications target the serotonin system to regulate mood and may alleviate symptoms like depression and anxiety. However, SSRIs have various side effects and do not address the underlying trauma, offering symptomatic relief rather than a path toward comprehensive healing.

Psilocybin-Assisted Therapy

In contrast, psilocybin-assisted therapy has shown promise in addressing the symptoms and underlying trauma by promoting neuroplasticity and facilitating profound emotional and existential experiences. Moreover, psilocybin sessions are usually fewer in number but longer in duration, potentially offering quicker, more sustained relief. The experience also tends to be more emotionally intense, allowing for a deep emotional processing not commonly achieved in traditional therapies.

Eye Movement Desensitization and Reprocessing (EMDR)

EMDR is another therapy used to treat PTSD, involving bilateral stimulation, often guided eye movements. While effective for some, EMDR focuses on reprocessing specific traumatic events and may not fully address the broader emotional and psychological aspects of trauma.

Prolonged Exposure Therapy

This approach is based on facing fears by having individuals with PTSD repeatedly recount their traumatic experience and confront trauma-related objects, activities, or situations they have avoided. While effective in reducing avoidance behaviors, the intensity of this approach can be overwhelming for some patients and may lead to dropouts.

Medicinal Cannabis

Some individuals turn to medicinal cannabis for symptom relief, given its potential to alleviate anxiety, improve sleep, and reduce nightmares. However, the psychoactive effects and potential dependency issues can make this a controversial option. Also, like SSRIs, it may provide symptomatic relief but not address the underlying issues.

Holistic Approaches (Yoga, Meditation, etc.)

Some people with PTSD have found relief through holistic methods like yoga, mindfulness meditation, and acupuncture. These approaches focus on mind-body integration and can effectively reduce anxiety and improve emotional regulation. However, they are usually considered complementary to other treatments and not as standalone solutions for PTSD.

Virtual Reality Exposure Therapy

Emerging technology has enabled simulated environments where individuals can confront traumatic events in a controlled setting.

Initial findings are promising but limited by the technology's accessibility and the lack of long-term studies.

Given the multifaceted nature of PTSD, combining psilocybin-assisted therapy with traditional treatments like Cognitive Behavioral Therapy (CBT) or mindfulness-based interventions could offer a comprehensive treatment strategy. This integrated approach has the potential to draw from the strengths of each modality, offering both immediate symptom relief and longer-term emotional and cognitive restructuring. Psilocybin could work synergistically with other treatments to amplify their benefits, such as enhancing the emotional breakthroughs achieved in CBT or boosting the awareness and emotional regulation that mindfulness practices facilitate. While the research is still developing, the possibility of an integrated treatment plan combining psilocybin with traditional therapies offers a promising avenue for future investigation.

The Significance of Mystical and Profound Experiences

The therapeutic benefits of magic mushrooms in treating PTSD are often significantly augmented by mystical or profoundly transformative experiences. These episodes can act as catalysts for enduring personal growth, emotional rehabilitation, and shifts in one's outlook on life.

Ego Dissolution: A common outcome of psychedelic experiences is the temporary dissolution of the ego or the sense of individual self. This phenomenon frequently induces a sensation of unity or interconnectedness with the surrounding world. For those grappling with PTSD, this shift can reframe their traumatic history as a singular chapter in a broader life story, rather than as an all-encompassing defining element.

Spiritual Revelations: Psilocybin can induce intense spiritual awakenings that imbue individuals with a renewed sense of purpose, meaning, and cosmic interconnectedness. This spiritual grounding can be an invaluable resource for those struggling with existential despair or feelings of hopelessness related to their PTSD.

Emotional Epiphanies: Navigating a psychedelic journey often culminates in periods of deep emotional unburdening and clarity. For PTSD sufferers, this can translate into the healing confrontation of long-repressed emotions like fear, sorrow, and rage, ultimately paving the way for emotional catharsis and recovery.

Heightened Self-Understanding: The reflective qualities of magic mushrooms provide a conducive environment for critical self-reflection. This clarity can empower individuals to identify and alter maladaptive thought patterns and behaviors, enhancing their coping strategies and overall mental well-being.

Enduring Positive Transformations: Many individuals report lasting beneficial alterations in their mental state and life circumstances following mystical or transformative psilocybin experiences. These enduring changes can manifest as improved mental health, enriched interpersonal relationships, a deeper appreciation for life, and a measurable decrease in PTSD symptoms.

Mystical and transformative experiences are fleeting moments and often serve as pivotal points in one's therapeutic journey. The insights gained from these profound states can provide a framework for continued healing, offering both immediate relief and long-term strategies for managing PTSD symptoms.

The right mindset and setting, often called 'set and setting' in psychedelic research, significantly influence the outcome. Factors like the individual's emotional state, the environment in which the experience occurs, and even the presence of a trained guide can make a considerable difference. The experience may yield the desired therapeutic benefits with a proper set and setting and could be counterproductive.

Each individual's experience with psilocybin therapy will be unique. Mystical and transformative states are complex phenomena influenced by many factors, including one's personal history, spiritual beliefs, and the severity of PTSD symptoms. While these experiences have shown promise in facilitating healing, they are not a one-size-fits-all solution.

When mystical and transformative experiences occur, they can serve as powerful catalysts for personal growth and emotional healing for those affected by PTSD.

Microdosing for PTSD

In this chapter, we delve into the use of microdosing magic mushrooms as a potential therapeutic approach for individuals struggling with PTSD. By taking sub-perceptual doses of psychedelic substances, individuals may experience subtle yet meaningful improvements in their mental health without undergoing the powerful and immersive effects of a full psychedelic journey.

We will discuss the various ways in which microdosing may help alleviate PTSD symptoms, as well as address potential challenges and concerns associated with this practice. Additionally, we will consider the practical aspects of implementing a microdosing regimen, including dosage, frequency, and duration, to ensure a safe and practical experience.

As we explore the potential of microdosing magic mushrooms for PTSD, we aim to provide valuable insights and guidance for those considering this innovative approach to healing and personal growth. This chapter will enable individuals with PTSD and their support networks to make well-informed decisions about the suitability of microdosing as a therapeutic option tailored to their needs and circumstances.

What is Microdosing?

Microdosing is consuming tiny, sub-perceptual doses of a psychedelic substance. Unlike a full psychedelic experience, microdosing intends to achieve subtle yet meaningful benefits without altering one's state of consciousness dramatically. This practice has seen a significant surge of interest in scientific circles and the general public.

In magic mushrooms, microdosing often involves taking a fraction of the dose that would induce a full psychedelic experience. Specifically, the doses are kept intentionally low, generally around 1/10th to 1/20th of a standard recreational dose. The aim is to minimize alterations in perception, cognition, or emotional state while maximizing potential benefits.

Over the years, microdosing has gained traction for its various applications. While its therapeutic effects are still under investigation, many individuals who microdose report incremental improvements in areas such as mood, focus, and creativity. These anecdotal reports suggest that microdosing could offer an alternative approach to enhancing mental well-being and cognitive function without the more intense, immersive effects of a full psychedelic session.

Potential Benefits and Applications

Microdosing with magic mushrooms has been reported to provide various potential benefits for individuals dealing with PTSD or other mental health challenges. Some of the commonly reported benefits and applications include:

Improved mood and emotional stability: Many individuals who practice microdosing find that it helps to alleviate symptoms of depression, anxiety, and emotional dysregulation, leading to a more stable and positive mood throughout the day.

Enhanced focus and cognitive function: Some users report increased concentration, mental clarity, and problem-solving abilities while microdosing, which can be particularly helpful for those struggling with cognitive difficulties related to PTSD.

Increased creativity and openness: Microdosing has been associated with enhanced creative thinking, making it an appealing option for artists, writers, or anyone seeking a boost in their creative pursuits.

Reduced symptoms of PTSD: For individuals dealing with PTSD, microdosing may help alleviate specific symptoms, such as intrusive thoughts, emotional numbness, or hypervigilance, by promoting a sense of calm and mental clarity.

Personal growth and self-discovery: Many people find that microdosing facilitates introspection and self-reflection, allowing them to gain insights into their thought patterns and behaviors, which can contribute to personal growth and healing.

It is important to note that individual experiences with microdosing can vary significantly, and not everyone will experience the same benefits. Additionally, more research is needed to understand the potential applications and benefits of microdosing for individuals with PTSD and other mental health challenges.

Commonly Used Substances

When it comes to microdosing for PTSD, the most common substance used is psilocybin, the active compound found in magic mushrooms. Psilocybin has shown promising results in research studies and anecdotal reports for its potential to alleviate PTSD symptoms and promote overall mental well-being. Several strains of magic mushrooms contain varying levels of psilocybin, such as Psilocybe cubensis, Psilocybe azurescens, and Psilocybe semilanceata, among others.

Other substances that are occasionally used for microdosing, although not specifically for PTSD, include:

LSD (Lysergic acid diethylamide): A powerful synthetic psychedelic, LSD has been reported to provide similar benefits to psilocybin when used in microdoses, including increased focus, mood improvement, and enhanced creativity. However, research on LSD microdosing for PTSD is limited compared to psilocybin.

Mescaline: Found in several species of cacti, such as the Peyote and San Pedro, mescaline is a naturally occurring psychedelic substance. While less common than psilocybin or LSD, some individuals have experimented with microdosing mescaline for its potential mood-enhancing and introspective effects.

It's important to note that the legal status of these substances varies widely depending on the country or region. Always comply with local laws and regulations before considering microdosing with any psychedelic substance. Additionally, each substance has unique effects, so it's essential to do thorough research and, if possible, consult with a knowledgeable professional before beginning a microdosing regimen.

Preparing for Your Microdosing Journey

Before starting a microdosing regimen for PTSD, preparing thoroughly to maximize safety and efficacy is imperative. Begin by setting clear intentions; whether you aim to reduce PTSD symptoms, improve emotional resilience, or elevate overall well-being, having a focused goal can keep you motivated. If you're already receiving medical treatment for PTSD, consult your healthcare provider to discuss your microdosing plans and to get advice on any potential interactions with other medications or therapies you may be undergoing.

Quality control is equally important. Make sure to source your psychedelic substances from reliable vendors, and if possible, test them for purity and potency to ensure you're getting what you expect. Your environment will also play a significant role in your experience, so set up a comfortable and consistent daily routine and have a support network.

Once your preparations are complete, develop a tailored microdosing schedule that outlines the dosage, frequency, and duration of your regimen. To gauge the effectiveness of your microdosing journey, keep a detailed journal or log to track changes in your symptoms, mood, or general well-being. A thorough preparation can improve the likelihood of a positive experience and help you get the most benefit for your PTSD symptoms and mental health.

Microdosing Protocols and Schedules

When it comes to microdosing for PTSD, there is no one-size-fits-all approach. Experts and practitioners have developed various protocols and schedules, and finding the one that works best for you is essential. Here are some popular microdosing protocols to consider:

The Fadiman Protocol: Named after Dr. James Fadiman, is a well-known and widely used microdosing regimen. This protocol advocates taking a microdose of a psychedelic substance on Day 1, followed by two days of abstinence (Days 2 and 3), and then resuming microdosing on Day 4. This cycle is repeated, with microdoses taken once every three days.

The rationale behind this schedule is to ensure that the body and mind have ample time to rest and integrate the effects of each microdose. By allowing for a two-day break between doses, individuals can avoid building a tolerance to the substance and minimize the risk of potential side effects. Furthermore, this schedule enables users to observe and assess the impact of microdosing on their mental, emotional, and physical well-being over an extended period.

Adhering to the Fadiman Protocol can help individuals maximize the potential benefits of microdosing while minimizing risks. This approach provides a structured and balanced microdosing regimen that can be safely incorporated into one's daily routine, fostering personal growth and well-being in a controlled and manageable manner.

The Stamets Stack: Designed by the esteemed mycologist Paul Stamets, is an alternative microdosing schedule that emphasizes a more frequent dosing pattern. In this protocol, individuals take a microdose every day for five consecutive days, followed by a two-day break. The purpose of the two-day hiatus is to avert tolerance buildup and provide an opportunity for integration of the microdosing experience.

Paul Stamets is not only known for his expertise in the field of fungi but also his innovative ideas regarding the use of psilocybin and other compounds for mental health and cognitive enhancement. The Stamets Stack is unique in that it often incorporates other natural supplements, such as lion's mane mushroom and niacin, which are believed to work synergistically with psilocybin to optimize brain function and overall well-being.

The daily microdosing in the Stamets Stack can lead to more consistent exposure to the substance, potentially providing more stable and ongoing benefits for individuals with PTSD. However, monitoring one's response to this protocol closely is essential, as the increased frequency of dosing may not be suitable for everyone. By following the Stamets Stack, users can explore a different microdosing approach that may be more effective for their particular needs and circumstances while ensuring a structured and safe regimen.

In addition to recommending the specific dosing schedule for the Stamets Stack, Paul Stamets also advises incorporating certain natural supplements to enhance the overall benefits of the microdosing experience. The combination of substances he proposes is often called the "Stamets Stack."

Stamets suggests combining the psilocybin microdose with two other supplements: lion's mane mushroom (Hericium erinaceus) and niacin (vitamin B3). Lion's mane mushroom is believed to support cognitive function, neurogenesis, and overall brain health. Niacin is a vasodilator, which helps increase blood flow and circulation in the body, potentially aiding in the distribution and efficacy of the psilocybin and lion's mane.

The idea behind this synergistic combination is that each substance contributes to enhancing cognitive function and promoting neuroplasticity, working together to optimize the overall benefits of the microdosing experience. By including lion's mane and niacin, the Stamets Stack aims to create a more comprehensive and practical approach to microdosing for individuals seeking cognitive and mental health benefits, including those with PTSD.

The 1-1-1 Protocol: The 1-1-1 Protocol, which consists of alternating microdosing days with rest days, allows individuals to experience the potential benefits of microdosing more consistently throughout the week while offering an opportunity for integration and preventing excessive exposure to the substance. This microdosing pattern can help individuals maintain a balanced state of mind, as the effects of the microdose may carry over into the rest of the day.

By following the 1-1-1 Protocol, individuals may find it easier to observe the subtle effects of microdosing on their mood, cognitive function, and overall well-being, as they have a shorter interval between doses. This can be particularly useful for those seeking relief from PTSD symptoms, as the more frequent dosing schedule may provide sustained support for emotional regulation and resilience.

Additionally, the 1-1-1 Protocol allows for greater flexibility and can be adjusted based on personal preferences or individual responses to microdosing. For example, if someone finds the effects too intense or experiences unwanted side effects, they can easily modify the protocol by extending the rest period or reducing the microdose amount.

The Balanced Protocol: The Balanced Protocol offers a unique approach to microdosing that combines the benefits of more frequent dosing with sufficient rest periods to promote optimal results. By microdosing on Days 1-4, individuals can experience the potential positive effects of magic mushrooms on mood, cognition, and PTSD symptoms more consistently, while still allowing their system to reset during the three-day break.

This dosing pattern can be particularly beneficial for those who want to maintain a steady routine and reap the potential advantages of microdosing throughout the workweek, with weekends reserved for rest and integration. The three-day break also helps to minimize the risk of developing a tolerance to the substance, ensuring that the microdoses remain effective over time.

The Balanced Protocol can be customized based on individual needs and preferences. For instance, if someone finds four consecutive days of microdosing too intense, they can adjust the protocol to include an additional rest day in between or decrease the microdose amount.

Travis Eric's Protocol: The Travis Eric Protocol is an unconventional approach to microdosing that emphasizes "filling up" the body with mushrooms by taking microdoses more frequently throughout the day and week. This protocol involves microdosing 5-7 days a week and taking doses in the morning, afternoon, and sometimes at night. As tolerance builds, the dosage is increased slightly to accommodate the body's adaptation to the substance.

With this approach, the effects of microdosing may become less predictable overall. However, after a month or two, individuals might notice a decreased desire for microdosing altogether. At this point, listening to the body and taking a break for a week or more is essential. After the "filling up" period, the need for microdosing may further diminish, and the microdoses' impact could increase, leading individuals to dose only once or twice a week or less.

The Travis Eric Protocol offers an alternative method for those who wish to explore the potential benefits of microdosing with a more intensive approach. However, it's crucial to be aware of the risks associated with more frequent dosing and carefully monitor one's response to this regimen.

Customized schedules: Some individuals may prefer to develop a personalized plan based on their unique needs, symptoms, and response to microdosing. Microdose on specific week days, such as Monday, Wednesday, and Friday, or adjust the frequency and duration based on your experiences and progress.

Pay attention to any emotional experiences, new sensitivities you might encounter, and the heightened awareness you may develop about yourself and others. As the mushrooms work to harmonize and heal your heart and mind, you'll likely become more attuned to your inner self and the world around you.

As with any microdosing protocol, consulting with a healthcare professional or an experienced guide when considering microdosing for PTSD is highly recommended. Prioritize self-care and listen to your body and mind throughout the microdosing journey to ensure a safe and beneficial experience.

Remember that microdosing is a highly individualized process, and it may take some trial and error to find the most effective protocol and schedule for you. Be patient, track your experiences, and adjust to optimize your microdosing journey for PTSD relief and overall well-being.

Troubleshooting Common Challenges

Microdosing can be a powerful tool for managing PTSD symptoms, but it is not without potential challenges. Here are some common issues that you may encounter and suggestions for troubleshooting them:

Insufficient effects: If you're not experiencing the desired benefits from microdosing, consider adjusting your dosage or protocol. Finding the right balance for your unique needs may take some experimentation. Remember to increase the dosage incrementally and allow enough time to assess the effects before making further adjustments.

Overstimulation or anxiety: Some individuals may find that microdosing exacerbates anxiety or causes overstimulation. If this occurs, try reducing your dosage or changing the frequency of your microdosing schedule. Incorporating stress-reducing activities like mindfulness practices or gentle exercise into your routine may also help mitigate these side effects.

Tolerance build-up: If you notice diminishing returns from your microdosing regimen, it could be due to tolerance build-up. To counteract this, try taking a break from microdosing for a week or two or experiment with different protocols that include more rest days between doses.

Difficulty integrating insights: Some people may need help incorporating the insights and lessons gained through microdosing into their daily lives. Regular journaling, meditation, or working with a supportive therapist can facilitate integration and personal growth.

Remember that microdosing is a personal journey, and it may take time to fine-tune your approach for optimal results. Stay patient, remain open to change, and seek support from the community or professionals when needed.

Personal Experiences and Case Studies

Exploring the lived experiences of those who have found relief through microdosing can be deeply illuminating. The following case studies highlight how microdosing has positively impacted individuals with PTSD. Through these narratives, we gain valuable insights into how this practice can help manage symptoms, foster emotional well-being, and encourage personal development.

John's journey: John's odyssey toward healing is a powerful testament to the potential benefits of microdosing psilocybin mushrooms for individuals grappling with PTSD. For years, John felt trapped by the debilitating symptoms of his condition—crippling anxiety, mood swings, and intrusive memories that sabotaged his peace of mind. Traditional therapies offered partial relief but never addressed the root of his distress. Feeling cornered and almost hopeless, John decided to explore the realm of psychedelic microdosing.

Upon initiating his microdosing regimen, John immediately noticed subtle but significant improvements. His anxiety levels started to decrease, making room for moments of calmness and mental clarity he had not experienced for years. The cloud of persistent low mood also began to lift, replaced by a more optimistic outlook and a tremendous enthusiasm for life.

Perhaps most striking was the change in how John interacted with his traumatic memories. Microdosing gave him a new emotional vocabulary, a fresh way to articulate, understand, and even integrate these haunting experiences. Instead of flashbacks that triggered panic, these memories assumed a narrative quality, as if they were stories that happened to him but did not define him. This newfound ability to process his trauma changed his internal emotional landscape and how he managed external stressors in his day-to-day life.

Over time, John found himself increasingly resilient. Tasks and events that would have previously sent his stress levels skyrocketing were now manageable. He described this shift as gaining a kind of "emotional armor"—not a barrier to numb him, but a form of resilience that allowed him to navigate life's challenges with greater ease and less dread.

While uniquely his own, John's journey offers hope and tangible evidence of how microdosing psilocybin mushrooms can serve as a valuable adjunct to traditional PTSD therapies. It illustrates the transformative potential that this emerging field holds for countless others who are desperately searching for relief.

Sarah's story: Sarah's experience adds another compelling layer to the mosaic of how microdosing psilocybin mushrooms can assist those battling with PTSD. As a military veteran, Sarah was all too familiar with the dark undertow of depression and anxiety that often accompany this condition. Despite participating in traditional therapy for her PTSD, she found herself stuck, as though she was treading emotional water without making any meaningful progress. It was during this plateau of treatment that Sarah decided to explore the world of microdosing as an adjunct to her existing therapies.

Within the first few weeks of her microdosing regimen, Sarah began recognizing an elevated self-awareness. It was as if a fog had lifted, enabling her to see her emotional and psychological landscapes with newfound clarity. She described it as having an elevated 'bird's-eye view' of her own life, allowing her to identify patterns and triggers she'd previously been blind to.

This increased self-awareness led to another significant discovery: Sarah began to comprehend better the underlying factors contributing to her PTSD. She could delve deeper into the root causes of her symptoms, such as the ingrained survival mechanisms that were now manifesting as hypervigilance and anxiety in her civilian life. She started to grasp the depth and complexity of her emotional scars, and how they were intricately tied to her service in the military.

With this newfound understanding, Sarah found her subsequent therapy sessions much more fruitful. Her interactions with her therapist shifted from somewhat superficial dialogues to penetrating conversations touching the core of her trauma. For the first time, she felt like she was not just managing her symptoms but actively engaging in deep emotional and psychological healing—the integrative approach—combining microdosing with traditional therapy—proved to be a game-changer for her.

Sarah's narrative not only exemplifies the transformational power of microdosing in addressing PTSD but also underscores its potential to amplify the effectiveness of established therapeutic modalities. Her story makes us optimistic about the synergistic future of integrating emerging treatments like microdosing with conventional mental health care for comprehensive, more effective healing.

Michael's transformation: Michael's account adds an essential perspective to the collection of personal journeys that illuminate how microdosing can serve as a lifeline for those grappling with PTSD. His traumatic experience was not born from combat or a violent event but stemmed from a catastrophic car accident that left him physically unscathed but emotionally and mentally shattered. Despite undergoing conventional treatments like cognitive behavioral therapy and pharmacotherapy, the grip of PTSD remained unyielding. Frustrated and desperate for relief, Michael ventured into microdosing as a last resort.

Almost immediately upon initiating his microdosing regimen, Michael found that the frequency and intensity of his PTSD symptoms, like intrusive thoughts and emotional numbing, began to diminish. Moreover, he noticed that the once-harrowing task of simply navigating daily life became less burdensome. The most significant change, however, was not just the symptom relief but a surprising secondary outcome—the emergence of an enthusiastic interest in mindfulness and meditation.

Within weeks of beginning his microdosing journey, Michael felt a newfound mental clarity and an innate pull towards mindfulness practices. Intrigued, he decided to incorporate mindfulness meditation into his daily routine. This was a turning point. As he combined microdosing with consistent meditation, Michael discovered that the two were remarkably synergistic. His sessions of quiet mindfulness deepened the benefits he was getting from microdosing, like a feedback loop that kept intensifying his emotional stability and awareness.

As time progressed, Michael delved deeper into mindfulness practices, including breathwork and body scan techniques. These activities became the cornerstones of his emotional well-being and served as valuable tools for self-regulation. Meditation and microdosing enabled him to cultivate a profound inner peace and resilience that he had never felt before. Over time, the debilitating memories of the car accident began to lose their potency, becoming less like insurmountable walls and more like challenges he had the tools to face and overcome.

Michael's transformation is a testimony to the powerful benefits of combining microdosing with complementary therapeutic practices. It underscores the potential of an integrative approach to healing—one that incorporates the strengths of cutting-edge and time-honored therapies. His story highlights the rich, untapped potential for layered treatments in the ongoing quest to find practical solutions for the multifaceted challenges of PTSD.

Emily's Revival: For Emily, a first responder who faced daily exposure to traumatic events, PTSD had become an unwelcome occupational hazard. Over the years, she developed intense feelings of hypervigilance, constant fatigue, and an oppressive emotional numbness. While her career involved saving lives, she felt her own life was slipping through her fingers. Traditional treatments like exposure therapy and prescription medications had some effect but failed to address the persistent emptiness she felt. As someone trained in emergency medicine, microdosing psychedelics seemed unconventional, even radical, but her yearning for a deeper form of healing led her to take the plunge.

As Emily began her microdosing journey, one of the first things she noticed was an increase in mental acuity. Her focus sharpened, allowing her to perform her demanding job with heightened precision. But the most profound changes were emotional. She started feeling the 'edges' of her emotions again as if the numbness was melting away, layer by layer. The wall she had built around herself to cope with daily trauma began to crumble, revealing a more vulnerable and authentic version of herself.

About a month into her regimen, Emily began to couple microdosing with expressive art therapy, a decision inspired by her newfound emotional openness. She found that art provided a non-verbal outlet for processing complex emotions that were often too overwhelming to confront directly. As she painted, sketched, and even sculpted, she felt she was externalizing the tangled web of emotions and memories that had resided in her for years, transforming them into something tangible, something manageable.

What was remarkable was how well microdosing and art therapy seemed to synergize. The microdosing appeared to unlock emotional doors within her, while art therapy served as a therapeutic channel through which those emotions could flow and be processed. The artwork became a visual journal of her inner landscape, reflecting her struggles and progress. Over time, her art began to shift, featuring brighter colors and more harmonious compositions, mirroring her internal transformation.

Emily's story adds another layer to our understanding of the multi-dimensional benefits of microdosing for PTSD. It emphasizes the importance of combining the biological and emotional recalibrations offered by microdosing with other forms of expressive and therapeutic activities. Her experience shows that there is no one-size-fits-all approach to healing, but rather an array of tools uniquely tailored to each individual's journey. It serves as an inspirational blueprint for others, revealing the untapped possibilities at the intersection of modern science and creative expression.

These personal accounts highlight the diverse ways in which microdosing can positively impact the lives of those living with PTSD. While each individual's experience will be unique, these stories offer hope and inspiration for others seeking alternative methods to heal and grow.

Macrodosing for PTSD

In this chapter, we explore the potential of macrodosing magic mushrooms as a therapeutic approach for individuals with PTSD. Throughout the chapter, we will discuss the benefits and applications of this approach, while emphasizing the importance of set and setting for a successful session.

We will also delve into the crucial role of integration and aftercare in maintaining the positive effects of a macrodosing experience. By highlighting personal stories and case studies, we aim to demonstrate the transformative potential of macrodosing in the context of PTSD treatment.

By examining the various aspects of macrodosing magic mushrooms for PTSD, we hope to provide a comprehensive understanding of this approach, allowing individuals and their support networks to make informed decisions about its potential role in their healing journey.

What is Macrodosing?

Macrodosing refers to consuming larger, often psychedelic-level doses of a substance, such as magic mushrooms, to induce significant psychological and emotional experiences. These experiences can be characterized by altered states of consciousness, vivid visualizations, heightened emotions, and intensified sensory perception.

Unlike microdosing, which involves taking sub-perceptual doses to enhance daily functioning, macrodosing aims to facilitate deep introspection, profound insights, and transformative experiences that can lead to lasting change and healing. Some individuals may encounter mystical or spiritual experiences during macrodosing sessions, contributing to a greater sense of interconnectedness, empathy, and personal growth.

In the context of PTSD treatment, macrodosing can help individuals confront and process unresolved trauma, foster emotional breakthroughs, and create a shift in perspective that promotes resilience and well-being. Macrodosing sessions can provide a safe and therapeutic space for individuals to explore their inner world and understand the root causes of their suffering.

It's important to note that macrodosing can be intense and unsuitable for everyone. Proper preparation, guidance, and integration ensure a safe and beneficial experience. Working with a knowledgeable practitioner or therapist specializing in psychedelic-assisted therapy can help maximize the potential benefits of macrodosing for individuals seeking relief from PTSD symptoms.

Potential Benefits and Applications

Macrodosing magic mushrooms for PTSD treatment has shown promising results in various clinical studies and anecdotal reports. The potential benefits and applications of macrodosing in the context of PTSD include:

Emotional breakthroughs: Macrodosing can help individuals access and process deeply buried emotions, facilitating emotional release and healing. This can lead to a greater understanding of one's trauma and help individuals work through unresolved issues.

Enhanced self-awareness: Intense psychedelic experiences can increase self-awareness, enabling individuals to understand better their triggers, emotional patterns, and defense mechanisms. This newfound self-awareness can contribute to more effective coping strategies and improved mental health.

Trauma processing: Macrodosing can create a safe space for individuals to confront and process traumatic memories, allowing them to reframe their experiences and integrate them into their lives healthier.

Improved mood and well-being: Many individuals report lasting improvements in mood, reduced anxiety, and an enhanced sense of well-being following macrodosing sessions. These positive changes can lead to greater resilience against the symptoms of PTSD.

Connection and empathy: Macrodosing can foster a sense of connection to others and the world, promoting empathy and compassion. This can help counter feelings of isolation and disconnection often experienced by individuals with PTSD.

Spiritual growth: Some individuals experience profound spiritual or mystical experiences during macrodosing sessions, which can contribute to a sense of purpose, meaning, and inner peace.

Lasting change: Macrodosing has the potential to create lasting changes in thought patterns, beliefs, and behaviors that contribute to PTSD symptoms. These shifts can lead to long-term improvements in mental health and overall well-being.

It's essential to recognize that macrodosing is not a one-size-fits-all solution and may not be suitable for everyone. The intensity of the experience can be overwhelming for some individuals, and adequate preparation, guidance, and integration support are essential for maximizing the potential benefits of macrodosing in treating PTSD.

Set and Setting for Macrodosing Sessions

Understanding and carefully considering set and setting is vital for anyone planning to undergo a macrodosing session with magic mushrooms, particularly for the treatment of PTSD. The term 'set' pertains to one's mental and emotional disposition going into the experience. It encompasses attitudes, thoughts, and feelings, while 'setting' refers to the physical and interpersonal environment where the psychedelic session occurs. Below are some fundamental considerations to help shape a meaningful and safe macrodosing session.

A constructive mindset going into the macrodosing experience is critical. It's beneficial to address any apprehensions or worries and establish an explicit purpose or intention for the session. Being open to facing potentially uncomfortable emotions or memories that could surface is part of the therapeutic process. The readiness to let go and trust the substance and the setting is often key to achieving meaningful therapeutic outcomes.

Your chosen physical environment for the macrodosing session should be a sanctuary that feels both safe and comfortable. Remove any potential sources of distraction or stress to allow for complete focus on the inner journey ahead. Creating a serene atmosphere with mellow lighting, tranquil music, or aromatic scents can significantly enhance the experience.

The social milieu is equally crucial. Having a knowledgeable and trusted guide or sitter accompany you during the session is generally advisable. This person should be versed in the intricacies of the psychedelic experience and capable of offering emotional reassurance and logistical support when needed. Their presence can be invaluable in helping you navigate the emotional and perceptual shifts that occur during the experience.

Choosing the right time for your macrodosing session is another significant aspect. Ensure you are free from pressing obligations before and after the session, enabling you to enter the experience without external stressors and to allocate time for reflection and integration afterward.

In the days preceding the macrodosing session, engage in practices that foster well-being and mental clarity, like meditation, journaling, physical exercise, or spending quality time in natural surroundings. These self-care activities help lay a favorable groundwork for the forthcoming psychedelic journey.

Post-session aftercare and integration are equally essential components. Reflecting on the experience is crucial, and you may find it helpful to write down your thoughts, talk them over with a trusted friend or therapist, or express yourself creatively. Mindfulness techniques can also assist in cementing the newfound perspectives or emotional shifts into your daily life.

By giving due diligence to both set and setting, you substantially heighten the odds of having a transformative, therapeutic macrodosing experience that could significantly contribute to your PTSD treatment.

Experiencing a Macrodosing Session: What to Expect

Embarking on a macrodosing journey with magic mushrooms can be profound and deeply transformative, especially for those seeking relief from PTSD. This guide offers an in-depth, chronological overview, unpacking the kaleidoscopic range of sensations and transformative phases one might undergo. Your initial interaction with the substance sets the stage for what promises to be an enlightening journey.

Within the 40- to 60-minute window post-consumption, a gentle lifting of the sensory veil commonly occurs. Your perception of the environment may gain newfound vividness, with colors appearing richer and emotionally laden nuances becoming palpable. If you've prepared your mushrooms as tea, anticipate this awakening to unfold more quickly; in contrast, ingestion with food might slightly protract this onset.

As you transition into the next pivotal stage of your journey—approximately 60 to 90 minutes in—you'll find yourself entering a transformative phase often referred to as 'the turning-over period.' At this moment, you may feel as if the very essence of the mushroom is making a personal, almost ceremonial introduction. Some users have described sensing the presence of unique beings or archetypes, such as an entity resembling a praying mantis or a multi-eyed winged angel.

This is a remarkably interactive segment of the experience, where both auditory and visual sensations reach new heights. Sounds may emerge without a clear source, enveloping you in an aural tapestry that defies explanation. With eyes closed, you might see intricate patterns or designs that dance and morph across your internal visual field. Physiological sensations are also amplified during this stage; you might experience a visceral 'stomach drop,' comparable to that sudden plunge on a roller coaster. Additional bodily reactions like yawning, nasal congestion, or brief bouts of stomach discomfort could occur, each serving as a harbinger of the mental and physical transformation underway. While these sensations can be startling initially, repeated experiences often lead to a greater appreciation for this brief yet profound phase, as it unfolds and transitions all too quickly.

Following the turning-over period, you find yourself fully immersed in what's colloquially known as 'the mushroom world.' Here, you have little control over the direction of your experience, akin to a passenger on an unpredictable yet enlightening journey. The term 'trip' is wholly appropriate, as you might find yourself navigating landscapes and narratives as vivid and complex as any foreign country you've visited. The feelings, visions, and lessons presented in this realm may range from blissful to unsettling, but it's crucial to remember the adage, "This too shall pass." A trip typically lasts 4 to 5 hours in total, leading you back to your familiar state of being, often incrementally.

In this otherworldly realm known as the "mushroom world," the landscapes and scenarios you encounter can vary widely but often share profound transformation and insight themes. For instance, some describe an "upside-down world," where it feels like you're walking beneath the surface of your everyday reality, seeing things from the vantage point of mycelium networks. This new perspective allows you to make novel connections, reassessing your life and your place in it from a unique angle.

Bad trips can occur, especially if you're not prepared to face the emotional and psychological intensity that psychedelics can unleash. The mushrooms have a knack for dissolving the mental compartments where we stash away fears, traumas, or memories we'd rather not confront. This can be unsettling, but also profoundly therapeutic, granting you the emotional fluidity to process these buried issues through more profound laughter or cries.

Some individuals recount an almost mythological transformation into their animal archetype. Imagine feeling like you've morphed into a lioness, entirely at ease in the dark, senses heightened and fully attuned to your environment. You might discover a newfound courage, symbolized by your ability to 'hiss' at fears that once held you captive.

The diversity of experiences in this mushroom-induced landscape ranges from deeply introspective to expansively insightful, and each 'destination' holds the potential for significant personal growth and emotional healing.

While in the mushroom world, your body may undergo a series of fascinating sensations that deepen your connection to your physical self and the natural environment. The urge to stretch can become almost irresistible as you become acutely aware of each muscle and fiber in your body. It's as if you can feel the very essence of your biological form, grounding you in a newfound appreciation for your physical existence. Many people also feel a strong pull to be outdoors, connecting with nature, as the heightened senses make the textures of leaves and the colors of the sky overwhelmingly vivid.

Conversely, you may be too sensitive to use electronic devices like phones or TVs. These technologies can become a source of distraction, pulling you away from the transformative journey you're on. It's essential to resist these diversions, focusing instead on mushrooms' organic and deeply personal insights. Additionally, caution is advised when introducing substances like cannabis during your trip. Though it might seem tempting, each substance has an entity, and combining entities can steer your experience in an entirely different direction, often adding layers of confusion rather than clarity to your journey.

As you traverse this world, your role is not to direct the experience but to surrender to it. Offering up resistance might steer the journey into a tumultuous course. Instead, adopt a posture of openness and curiosity; become an observer of your mind's theater. This lack of resistance and complete surrender could yield the most therapeutic outcomes—bringing buried emotions or subconscious thoughts to the surface for examination and potential integration.

Eventually, the experience will wane, and you'll settle back into your baseline reality. This is a critical juncture, sometimes compared to the awakening phase after a vivid and intricate dream. Your cognition will sharpen, your surroundings will begin to feel familiar again, and your sense of self will consolidate. The edges of your enhanced perceptions will soften, and as they do, you'll often find yourself enveloped in a state of calm and reflective poise.

This post-trip period is not merely a return to normalcy but a valuable stage for reflection and integration. The insights from your trip could offer profound revelations, which may be incredibly beneficial to your ongoing therapeutic journey for

PTSD or any other emotional or psychological challenges. Take this time to jot down your thoughts, engage in a heartfelt conversation with a trusted friend or a guide, or indulge in creative expression. These activities not only serve to anchor your experience but also provide a robust framework for you to revisit and interpret the rich tapestry of your journey.

Armed with this knowledge, you can better prepare for the transformative event that a macrodosing session promises to be, enriching your life in ways you might never have anticipated.

Exploring the Spectrum of Psilocybin Dosages

The amount of psilocybin mushrooms you ingest significantly impacts the nature of your psychedelic experience and its potential therapeutic outcomes. Understanding the dosage spectrum is crucial for tailoring an experience that meets your needs and intentions. For those new to psychedelics, "microdosing" involves taking around 1/10th to 2/10ths of a gram. These doses are sub-perceptual, enhancing mood and cognition without inducing hallucinations.

If you aim to immerse more deeply into the psychedelic realm, dosages typically begin at one gram, which offers a "gentle turning over" of awareness. Scaling upwards, 3-5 grams will lead you into profoundly emotional, cognitive, and hallucinatory realms. Renowned ethnobotanist Terence McKenna famously recommended a "heroic dose" of 5 grams, advising users to take it in a dark, quiet room to fully immerse themselves in the experience.

In psychedelic research, some claims and studies push the boundaries of what we understand about the capabilities of substances like psilocybin. One such claim suggests a study involving synthetic psilocybin dosages of 10 grams; paraplegic participants were purportedly able to regain their ability to walk after suggestions during the trip that they could use their legs. The explanation for this incredible phenomenon ranges from mental reprogramming to actual physical repair of neurons, almost as if a "glitch in the matrix" had been corrected. While this is an extraordinary claim that needs to be verified through rigorous scientific scrutiny, it highlights the possibilities that high doses of psilocybin may offer.

Kilindi Iyi advocates for extremely high dosages, recommending upwards of 60 grams for a more expansive and profound experience. Following Kilindi's footsteps, Mushroom Matt, also known as Matt Johnson, has explored further, reporting taking dosages as high as 110 grams. According to Matt, anything beyond 10 grams could be considered entering "god dose" territory. Past 30 grams, the experience becomes "interdimensional," suggesting that the visions and insights gained are no longer just amplifications or distortions of our reality, but perceptions of an entirely different dimension.

Matt offers another insight into the dosage-effect relationship. Whether you consume a moderate dose of 3.5 grams or venture into the high triple digits, the core message of the experience remains the same. What changes, he says, is the volume of the message, akin to the difference between a whisper and a shout.

To underscore the safety profile of psilocybin, Matt points out that even at these extreme dosages, he and others have returned without apparent physical harm. However, it's crucial to note that such high doses are not recommended for everyone, especially those new to psychedelics or with pre-existing mental health conditions. These uncharted territories have risks and should only be approached with ample preparation.

Higher doses of psilocybin mushrooms, especially those beyond 3 grams, can lead to intense experiences often accompanied by significant discomfort. Physically, you may encounter symptoms like nausea, vomiting, and visual distortions. On the psychological front, you might experience racing thoughts, out-of-body experiences, intense emotional upheavals, or a fundamental questioning of your perceived reality. Preparing for such potentially challenging experiences is highly advisable.

One effective way to prepare is by incorporating meditation into your routine. Meditation fosters mindfulness, which can help you maintain a sense of groundedness and presence during a trip. Other methods for cultivating a tolerance for discomfort include cold plunge therapy, participating in long-distance endurance races, and undergoing sweat lodge rituals. These practices can build physical resilience and train your mind to sit with discomfort, enhancing your psychological readiness for a higher-dose mushroom experience.

The key to managing these challenging moments during a trip is surrender. Fighting off the sensations or the altered state of consciousness can often exacerbate your discomfort. Instead, acknowledging the temporary nature of the experience can help. Remember, this too shall pass. Practicing acceptance and surrendering to the experience can significantly shape how you navigate the challenges that may arise. The less you resist, the more you allow the experience to unfold naturally, making it easier for you to glean insights and emerge on the other side of discomfort with greater clarity and understanding.

Integration and Aftercare

Integration and aftercare are essential to the healing process following a macrodosing session with magic mushrooms. These processes help you make sense of your experiences and apply the insights gained to your everyday life. Proper integration and aftercare can lead to lasting positive changes in your mental health, especially when treating PTSD. Consider the following strategies:

Reflect on the experience: Take time to process and contemplate the insights and emotions that arose during your macrodosing session. This may involve journaling, drawing, or simply engaging in quiet reflection. Try to identify any recurring themes or messages that emerged during the experience.

Seek support: Share your experience with a trusted friend, therapist, or support group. This can help you gain new perspectives, validate your emotions, and receive guidance on how to apply the insights to your life.

Develop new habits: Use the insights gained during your macrodosing session to inform changes in your daily life. This might involve adopting healthier habits, engaging in self-care practices, or addressing unresolved traumas or emotional issues.

Mindfulness and meditation: Regular mindfulness and meditation practices can help consolidate the benefits of your macrodosing experience. These practices can enhance self-awareness, emotional regulation, and resilience, which are critical for healing from PTSD.

Stay connected: Maintain contact with your support network, therapist, or psychedelic community. This can reinforce your commitment to healing and personal growth and provide ongoing support and encouragement.

Be patient: Healing from PTSD is a gradual process, and it's essential to be patient with yourself as you integrate the insights gained from your macrodosing session. Remember that true transformation often takes time, persistence, and self-compassion.

By focusing on integration and aftercare, you can maximize the therapeutic potential of your macrodosing experience and contribute to lasting healing from PTSD.

Personal Experiences and Case Studies

Personal experiences and case studies can offer valuable insights and perspectives on the real-world impact of macrodosing. Here, we present a few stories that illustrate the healing potential of magic mushrooms when addressing PTSD:

John's Transformation: John, a military veteran who had served in multiple combat zones, carried the weight of severe PTSD for years after returning from deployment. Terrifying nightmares marred his nights, and his days were filled with haunting flashbacks, leading to a downward spiral of debilitating anxiety and emotional turbulence. His relationships suffered, and his career stagnated as the traditional medications and therapies offered little relief.

In a final act of desperation, John decided to attend a therapeutic macrodosing retreat, which focused on using magic mushrooms as a form of treatment for PTSD. With a mixture of skepticism and hope, he entered the withdrawal, adhering closely to the guidelines regarding set and setting, and preparing himself mentally and emotionally for the experience.

During his macrodosing session, John felt as though he had journeyed through the labyrinth of his mind. He encountered memories he had walled off and emotions he had bottled up, but this time, he saw them through a different lens. It was as if he was guided by an unseen hand, providing him with insights and perspectives that he had never considered. He came face-to-face with his trauma, and for the first time, he didn't turn away. The experience was deeply emotional, sometimes tricky, but always enlightening.

As he returned to his ordinary consciousness, John felt a seismic shift within himself. His anxiety levels were markedly reduced, and his outlook on life had changed dramatically. The flashbacks and nightmares that had tormented him seemed to lose their grip, occurring less frequently and with reduced intensity. John credits not only the magic mushrooms but also the act of confronting his trauma and processing it in a therapeutic setting for his transformation.

He still has a journey ahead of him, but for the first time in years, it's a journey he looks forward to. Armed with new tools for emotional and psychological well-being and an increased sense of inner peace, John feels like he's finally started to reclaim his life. The macrodosing experience, for him, was not a magic bullet but a turning point that redirected the trajectory of his energy toward healing and wholeness.

Sarah's Journey to Healing: From a young age, Sarah had endured a childhood marred by abuse, the scars of which had seeped into her adult life, manifesting as PTSD. Despite engaging in years of traditional therapy, she often felt like she was only scratching the surface of her emotional pain. While therapy sessions and medications provided some relief, they seemed to act as mere band-aids, never fully addressing the deep-rooted trauma she carried within her.

Frustrated but not defeated, Sarah began exploring alternative therapeutic options. After thorough research and consultation with healthcare professionals, she opted to participate in a guided macrodosing session, tailored specifically for individuals struggling with PTSD. Approaching the session with cautious optimism, Sarah meticulously prepared her mindset and environment, following the recommended guidelines for a safe and transformative experience.

As the macrodosing session commenced, Sarah felt enveloped in a cascade of emotions and sensations she had never felt before.

For the first time, she entered an empathetic space that allowed her to confront her past without the overwhelming weight of shame or blame. During her journey, Sarah experienced a breakthrough moment—she felt she was enveloped in an aura of profound love and forgiveness. This transformative experience enabled her to reflect on her past trauma, not as a crippling force but as a chapter in her life that she could now close.

In that pivotal moment, it was as if years of emotional baggage were lifted off her shoulders. The experience provided her with a newfound capability to face her traumas, to forgive not just those who wronged her, but also herself for the years she had spent entangled in self-blame and loathing.

Returning to her regular state of consciousness, Sarah felt like a new person. The overwhelming fear and anxiety that had become her constant companions seemed to dissipate. She noticed a significant reduction in her PTSD symptoms, with fewer episodes of anxiety and a marked improvement in her overall well-being.

Though Sarah acknowledges that her healing journey is far from over, the macrodosing session served as a catalyst, propelling her into a new chapter of her life. She continues to attend therapy but now incorporates mindfulness and other holistic practices into her treatment. Empowered and more attuned to her emotional landscape, Sarah has rediscovered hope and the courage to continue her journey toward healing and self-discovery.

Michael's Transformation: A first responder by profession, Michael had always prided himself on being a person who could handle high-stakes situations. However, years of witnessing the raw, often harrowing realities of human suffering took a heavy toll on him. Over time, he found himself grappling with PTSD, haunted by vivid flashbacks and crippling anxiety that made it increasingly difficult to function both at work and at home.

Despite trying multiple treatment approaches—ranging from conventional medication and talk therapy to more experimental treatments—Michael found little to no relief. His symptoms seemed resistant to change, leaving him desperate and out of options. As a last resort, he explored macrodosing with magic mushrooms, driven by emerging evidence supporting its therapeutic benefits for PTSD sufferers.

Apprehensive yet hopeful, Michael approached the macrodosing session with an open mind. He made sure to consult experts and read up on guidelines for a secure and mindful experience. As he embarked on his journey, a shift occurred: the weight of his emotional armor began to lift, and he entered an altered state where his deeply rooted feelings of guilt and powerlessness surfaced as vivid, symbolic imagery.

During this eye-opening part of the session, Michael was confronted by powerful visual representations—scenes that wove together past experiences and emotions, laying bare the depths of his guilt and helplessness. For instance, he saw himself standing alone in a storm, burdened by the weight of a sinking ship that symbolized his perceived failures. The imagery was intense, but it was as if the mushrooms provided him with a compassionate lens to interpret and confront these emotions.

Armed with this newfound clarity, Michael began to understand that the guilt he felt was tied to unrealistic expectations of omnipotence; he had always thought that he should be able to save everyone and control every outcome, which was, in reality, impossible. The vivid imagery gave way to insights that made him reevaluate his understanding of responsibility and control, acknowledging his human limitations for the first time.

Michael felt like a fog had been lifted, emerging from the session. The tightly coiled ball of guilt and anxiety inside him had begun to unravel, leaving space for healing and emotional processing. The experience set in motion a profound change, allowing him to engage more constructively in therapy and adopt new coping strategies. He returned to work, not as the person burdened by unattainable expectations, but as someone with a greater sense of compassion—for the people he helps, and importantly, for himself.

While Michael recognizes that the journey ahead is long and fraught with challenges, the macrodosing session served as a transformative pivot point, offering him renewed hope and a more straightforward path toward emotional healing and self-acceptance.

Emily's Odyssey: Emily had always been the rock of her family, the dependable one who seemed unshakeable. However, years of battling depression and anxiety wore her down, casting a shadow over her life that she couldn't escape. Medications, while helpful, only provided temporary relief, and traditional therapies didn't offer her the depth of understanding she yearned for.

Out of options and nearing a point of despair, Emily began researching alternative treatments and discovered the potential benefits of macrodosing magic mushrooms for mental health conditions. Intrigued and cautiously optimistic, she consulted experts and decided to undergo a guided macrodosing session.

From the moment she ingested the mushrooms, Emily felt a sense of expectation, as if standing on the threshold of something momentous. The usual symptoms—her constant companions of worry and sadness—seemed to fade into the background as she stepped into a realm of heightened sensitivity and awareness.

During the peak of her experience, Emily was transported to what felt like an alternate universe, a tranquil forest where time and space lost their conventional meanings. She felt her body dissolve into the surroundings, experiencing a profound interconnectedness with nature. Each tree, each leaf seemed to pulse with life, resonating with her existence.

As she journeyed deeper into this ethereal world, Emily was confronted with a series of doors. Each door represented a facet of her life where she had felt stuck or in pain. Guided by an intuitive sense of knowing, she opened one that led to her childhood, unveiling long-suppressed memories of joy and wonder but also of insecurity and sorrow. In the safe embrace of this alternate realm, she felt equipped to revisit these memories without the dread and apprehension that usually accompanied them.

She realized the weight she had been carrying wasn't just her own but also the unspoken expectations and unhealed traumas of her family. It became apparent that her role as the 'rock' was both a blessing and a curse; it had given her purpose but also burdened her with responsibilities that were not hers to bear.

As Emily returned to reality, the forest and the doors fading into the ether, she felt lighter, as though years of emotional detritus had been swept away. She returned to her life not as the worn-down person always on the edge but as someone renewed, grounded, and profoundly changed.

This single macrodosing experience didn't solve all of Emily's problems, but it did give her the clarity and courage to confront them head-on. It became a turning point, equipping her with a different perspective and the emotional tools to engage with her challenges more constructively and compassionately. Finally, Emily felt hopeful, ready to navigate the complexities of her life with renewed strength and understanding.

These personal experiences and case studies highlight the potential of macrodosing magic mushrooms for treating PTSD. They underscore the importance of set and setting, integration, and aftercare, as well as the power of transformative experiences in promoting lasting healing. While each individual's journey is unique, these stories offer hope and inspiration for those seeking relief from PTSD through alternative treatments.

Enhancing the Effects of Magic Mushrooms

In this chapter, we will examine various methods and techniques that can augment the impact of magic mushrooms in addressing PTSD symptoms. Although microdosing and macrodosing can be potent tools individually, combining them with complementary practices and strategies can amplify their healing potential. By learning about and incorporating these approaches, you can develop a more comprehensive and personalized treatment plan, further fostering your healing and personal growth.

We will delve into the significance of set and setting, explore the advantages of microdosing for creativity and athletic performance, and discuss the role of integration practices in promoting enduring change. Collectively, these components can assist you in unlocking the full power of magic mushrooms, optimizing their influence on your PTSD recovery process.

Set and Setting Strategies

Here are some additional strategies to complement the set and setting guidelines previously discussed to enhance the healing potential of magic mushrooms for PTSD treatment.

Rituals and Symbolism: Incorporating personal rituals or symbols into your experience can help create a sense of reverence, intention, and focus. For example, you might light a candle, burn sage or incense, or create a small altar with meaningful objects. These rituals anchor your intentions and deepen your connection to the experience.

Nurturing the Senses: Engaging your senses can help make your environment more supportive and immersive. Consider incorporating comfortable blankets or cushions, nature sounds or calming music, and soothing scents like essential oils. These sensory inputs can contribute to a positive set and setting and enhance your overall experience.

Digital Detox: Disconnecting from digital devices before, during, and after your session can help create a more mindful and focused environment. Turning off your phone, computer, and other electronic devices can minimize distractions and allow you to be more present and attuned to your inner experience.

Mindful Movement: Incorporating gentle, mindful movement practices like yoga, tai chi, or stretching before or after your session can help ground you and facilitate a deeper connection to your body. Movement can release physical tension and help process emotions, making it a valuable adjunct to your magic mushroom experience.

Creative Expression: Engaging in creative activities like drawing, painting, writing, or playing music during the integration phase can help you process and make sense of your experience. Creative expression can also be a therapeutic tool, aiding in the healing process and offering new perspectives on your journey.

By integrating these additional strategies into your set and setting, you can further optimize the healing potential of magic mushrooms for PTSD treatment, creating a more profound and transformative experience.

Benefits of Microdosing for Creativity in the Context of PTSD Recovery

Microdosing magic mushrooms can profoundly affect creativity, which can play a significant role in the healing process for individuals with PTSD. By boosting creative thinking, problem-solving abilities, and emotional expression, microdosing can help those with PTSD find new perspectives on their trauma and foster resilience in their recovery journey.

Enhanced Creative Thinking: Microdosing can stimulate divergent thinking, generating multiple ideas and solutions to a problem. By promoting a more open and flexible mindset, individuals with PTSD can approach their trauma from different angles, gaining new insights and coping strategies.

Improved Emotional Expression: PTSD often results in numbness or difficulty expressing emotions. Microdosing can help break down barriers to emotional expression, allowing individuals to explore and process their feelings safely and constructively. Creative outlets such as writing, painting, or making music can provide a therapeutic way to express and process emotions related to trauma.

Connection to the Unconscious Mind: Microdosing can help bridge the gap between the conscious and unconscious mind, revealing hidden patterns and insights. This connection can lead to a deeper understanding of the roots of trauma and promote healing through self-discovery and personal growth.

Developing New Coping Mechanisms: By fostering creativity, microdosing can help individuals with PTSD develop novel coping mechanisms and build resilience. Creative activities can provide comfort and support during the healing process, providing a healthy outlet for stress and negative emotions.

Building a Supportive Creative Community: Engaging in creative activities can help connect with others with similar interests or experiences. This sense of community can provide emotional support and encouragement during recovery, further enhancing the benefits of microdosing for PTSD treatment.

By incorporating microdosing into a creative practice, individuals with PTSD can tap into the healing power of creativity and unlock new pathways for growth and recovery. Combining microdosing and creative expression can help create a more holistic and personalized treatment plan that addresses the unique needs and challenges faced by those with PTSD.

Benefits of Microdosing for Athletic Performance in the Context of PTSD Recovery

Microdosing magic mushrooms can also positively impact athletic performance, which can be particularly beneficial for individuals with PTSD. Regular physical activity has long been recognized as essential to mental health and well-being. By enhancing various aspects of athletic performance, microdosing can help those with PTSD develop a consistent exercise routine, which can, in turn, contribute to their overall healing process.

Increased Focus and Concentration: Microdosing can improve mental clarity and focus, allowing individuals to better engage in their chosen physical activities. This heightened concentration can lead to more effective workouts, improved skill development, and significant accomplishment.

Enhanced Mind-Body Connection: Microdosing can foster a deeper connection between the mind and body, promoting a greater awareness of physical sensations and movement patterns. This improved mind-body connection can lead to better form, technique, and overall performance in various athletic pursuits.

Boosted Energy and Endurance: Some individuals report increased energy levels and stamina when microdosing, allowing them to sustain their physical activity for extended periods. This boost in endurance can be particularly beneficial for those with PTSD, as regular exercise can help alleviate symptoms of depression, anxiety, and stress.

Improved Recovery and Resilience: Microdosing may enhance the body's natural recovery processes, reducing inflammation and promoting healing after physical exertion. This accelerated recovery can lead to more consistent training, greater resilience, and a reduced risk of injury.

Heightened Motivation and Enjoyment: Microdosing can increase motivation and overall enjoyment of physical activity, helping individuals with PTSD establish and maintain a regular exercise routine. Engaging in enjoyable physical activities can promote well-being, accomplishment, and self-efficacy, all of which can contribute to healing.

Incorporating microdosing into an athletic routine can help individuals with PTSD harness the benefits of regular physical activity, supporting their journey toward healing and personal growth. Combining microdosing with exercise can create a more comprehensive and tailored treatment plan that addresses the mental and physical aspects of PTSD recovery.

If you've found the insights in this section on the benefits of microdosing for athletic performance within the context of PTSD recovery intriguing, I highly recommend taking your understanding to the next level. The book 'The Athlete's Trip: Unleashing the Potential of Magic Mushrooms for Athletic Performance' offers a comprehensive guide that could be invaluable. This resource will deepen your knowledge and give you practical tools for incorporating mushrooms into your athletic routine for optimized performance. Don't miss out on this opportunity to enhance your physical and mental well-being in a truly revolutionary way.

The Role of Integration Practices in Facilitating Long-Lasting Change

Integration practices ensure that the insights and experiences gained from microdosing and macrodosing magic mushrooms lead to long-lasting, positive changes in individuals with PTSD. By actively processing and incorporating these insights into daily life, individuals can develop new habits, perspectives, and coping mechanisms that support their healing journey and contribute to their overall well-being.

Journaling: Writing about one's experiences and insights gained during microdosing or macrodosing sessions can help individuals process their thoughts and emotions, recognize patterns, and develop a deeper understanding of their inner workings. Journaling is also valuable for tracking progress and identifying areas requiring further attention or exploration.

Reflection and Meditation: Setting aside time for quiet reflection and meditation can allow individuals to explore their experiences, emotions, and insights on a deeper level. Mindfulness practices, such as meditation or breathwork, can help cultivate a greater self-awareness and emotional regulation, essential for long-term healing and growth.

Artistic and Creative Expression: Engaging in artistic or creative activities can provide a powerful means of processing and integrating one's experiences with magic mushrooms. Creative expression can take many forms, such as painting, drawing, music, dance, or writing. It can help individuals access and convey complex emotions or insights that may be difficult to express through words alone.

Therapy and Support: Working with a knowledgeable therapist or support group can provide valuable guidance and a safe space for discussing one's experiences and progress. These professional resources can offer targeted interventions, help individuals develop effective coping strategies, and support them in their ongoing integration process.

Nature and Mind-Body Practices: Spending time in nature and engaging in mind-body practices, such as yoga or tai chi, can facilitate the integration of experiences and insights gained from magic mushrooms. These practices can help individuals ground themselves, release stress, and connect more deeply with their inner wisdom and healing capabilities.

By actively engaging in integration practices, individuals can ensure that the benefits and insights gained from magic mushrooms are not just temporary but lead to lasting, positive change. These practices support the development of new perspectives, habits, and coping mechanisms that can empower individuals with PTSD to continue their healing journey and enhance their overall quality of life.

Legal and Safety Considerations

While the potential benefits of microdosing and macrodosing are promising, it's essential to understand and navigate the complex legal landscape surrounding using magic mushrooms. It's important to ensure safe and responsible use to minimize risks and maximize the therapeutic potential of these powerful substances.

We will explore the current legal status of magic mushrooms, which varies greatly depending on the country or region. We will also guide you on using magic mushrooms safely and responsibly, emphasizing the importance of set and setting, dosage, and the presence of a trusted sitter or guide. Finally, we will discuss potential drug interactions and contraindications to be aware of when considering using magic mushrooms for PTSD treatment.

By familiarizing yourself with the legal and safety considerations outlined in this chapter, you can make informed decisions about incorporating magic mushrooms into your healing journey, while mitigating potential risks and optimizing the therapeutic benefits.

The Current Legal Status of Magic Mushrooms

The legal status of magic mushrooms varies significantly worldwide and is subject to change as public opinion and scientific research evolve. It's essential to stay informed about the laws in your country or region, as the possession, cultivation, sale, or consumption of magic mushrooms may be regulated or prohibited.

In the United States, psilocybin-containing mushrooms are classified as a Schedule I substance under the Controlled Substances Act, making them illegal at the federal level. However, some cities and states have decriminalized or deprioritized the enforcement of laws related to psilocybin, such as Denver, Colorado, and Oregon.

In Canada, psilocybin mushrooms are also illegal, but exceptions have been granted for specific individuals to use psilocybin for medical purposes, such as end-of-life care. Additionally, a growing movement is advocating for the decriminalization and potential legalization of magic mushrooms for therapeutic purposes.

In Europe, the legal status of magic mushrooms varies widely from country to country. Some countries, like the Netherlands, have more lenient laws, where selling and consuming "magic truffles," which contain psilocybin, are allowed in designated "smart shops." In contrast, other countries maintain strict prohibitions on psilocybin-containing substances.

Researching and adhering to the laws in your location is crucial to avoid legal consequences. It's also important to stay updated on any changes to legislation, as the legal landscape surrounding magic mushrooms is continuously evolving. As more research emerges supporting the therapeutic potential of magic mushrooms for various mental health conditions, including PTSD, the legal status of these substances may change in the future.

Ensuring Safe and Responsible Use

To ensure the safe and responsible use of magic mushrooms, especially when considering their application for PTSD treatment, it's crucial to follow specific guidelines and best practices. These recommendations will help minimize potential risks and maximize the therapeutic benefits of your experience.

Education: Familiarize yourself with the effects, potential risks, and proper dosage of magic mushrooms. Research the experiences of others and consult reliable sources to make informed decisions about your use.

Sourcing: Obtain magic mushrooms from a trusted and reputable source to ensure purity and correct identification. The best way to source magic mushrooms is to grow your own. Often, their cultivation can be as healing as ingesting them.

Dosage: Start with a conservative dose, especially if you're new to magic mushrooms or microdosing. Monitor your body's response and adjust the dosage to achieve the desired effects while minimizing potential side effects.

Set and setting: As mentioned earlier, your mindset and environment shape your experience. Ensure you're in a positive mental state and a supportive, comfortable atmosphere when using magic mushrooms.

Support: Engage the help of a trusted friend, therapist, or guide, particularly for macrodosing sessions. Their presence can provide emotional support, guidance, and reassurance during your experience.

Health considerations: Be aware of any pre-existing mental or physical health conditions that may be contraindicated for magic mushroom use. Consult with a healthcare professional if you're unsure or have concerns about potential interactions or risks.

Integration: Following your experience, take the time to process, reflect, and integrate the insights and learnings you've gained. This can involve journaling, discussing your experience with a trusted individual, or engaging in mindfulness practices.

Legal awareness: Stay informed about the legal status of magic mushrooms in your location and adhere to the laws and regulations to avoid potential legal consequences.

By following these guidelines, you can ensure a safer, more responsible, and beneficial experience with magic mushrooms, allowing you to maximize your potential in addressing PTSD symptoms and facilitating personal growth.

Potential Drug Interactions and Contraindications

When considering magic mushrooms for PTSD treatment, it's essential to be aware of potential drug interactions and contraindications. Certain medications and health conditions may interact negatively with the active compounds in magic mushrooms, such as psilocybin and psilocin. To minimize risks and ensure a safe experience, take the following precautions:

Medication interactions: Some medications may interact with magic mushrooms, causing undesired effects or reducing efficacy. Notable interactions include:

- Antidepressants, particularly selective serotonin reuptake inhibitors (SSRIs) and monoamine oxidase inhibitors (MAOIs), can potentially lead to serotonin syndrome or weaken the effects of magic mushrooms.
- Antipsychotic medications may also interact with magic mushrooms, potentially worsening symptoms of mental health disorders or causing adverse reactions.
- Blood pressure medications, sedatives, or other medications that affect the central nervous system may interact with magic mushrooms and cause unwanted side effects.

If you take any medications, consult a healthcare professional before using magic mushrooms to avoid potential interactions.

Mental health conditions: Individuals with a personal or family history of psychotic disorders, such as schizophrenia or bipolar disorder, should exercise caution when using magic mushrooms. The psychedelic experience may exacerbate symptoms or trigger an episode in susceptible individuals.

Heart conditions: Magic mushrooms can cause temporary increases in blood pressure and heart rate. If you have a pre-existing heart condition, consult a healthcare professional before using magic mushrooms to ensure your safety.

Pregnancy and breastfeeding: The effects of magic mushrooms on fetal development and nursing infants are not well studied. It's recommended to avoid using magic mushrooms during pregnancy and while breastfeeding to minimize potential risks to the baby.

Allergies: Although rare, some individuals may be allergic to the compounds found in magic mushrooms or experience hypersensitivity reactions. If you have a history of allergies or hypersensitivity to other fungi or medications, consult a healthcare professional before using magic mushrooms.

Substance use disorders: Individuals with a history of substance use disorders should exercise caution when using magic mushrooms, as they may have a higher risk of developing psychological dependence or experiencing adverse reactions.

Mixing with other substances: Combining magic mushrooms with other psychoactive substances, such as alcohol, cannabis, or stimulants, can lead to unpredictable effects and increase the risk of adverse reactions. It's best to avoid mixing magic mushrooms with other substances to ensure a safe and controlled experience.

Individual factors: People respond differently to magic mushrooms, and factors such as age, weight, metabolism, and genetics can influence the experience. Start with a low dose and increase gradually to find the optimal dosage for your unique needs and circumstances.

By being aware of potential drug interactions, contraindications, and other safety concerns, you can make informed decisions about using magic mushrooms for PTSD treatment. Always consult a healthcare professional before starting any new treatment, and prioritize your safety and well-being.

Personal Stories and Case Studies

In this chapter, we delve into the personal stories and case studies of individuals who have found healing and transformation through magic mushrooms in their journey to overcome PTSD. These powerful narratives offer a glimpse into the real-world applications and potential of microdosing and macrodosing, providing inspiration and insight for those seeking alternative treatments for PTSD.

We will introduce diverse personal experiences, reflecting the unique challenges, triumphs, and insights gained from incorporating microdosing and macrodosing into their treatment plans. While each person's journey is distinctly their own, a common thread of hope, resilience, and transformation runs through these narratives. By sharing these personal experiences, we aim to foster a sense of connection and understanding, highlighting the power of magic mushrooms to facilitate profound healing and growth. As you read through these stories, we encourage you to keep an open mind and consider how these experiences might resonate with your journey toward healing from PTSD.

Story 1: Overcoming Trauma with Microdosing

James, a 34-year-old Army veteran, struggled with PTSD for years following his deployment to a war zone. His symptoms included flashbacks, nightmares, and debilitating anxiety that made it difficult for him to hold down a job and maintain relationships. Traditional therapies provided some relief, but James felt trapped in a cycle of fear and emotional pain.

James decided to try it after hearing about microdosing magic mushrooms from a friend. He began cautiously, taking a sub-perceptual dose of psilocybin every three days. Within a few weeks, he noticed a shift in his mindset and a reduction in the intensity of his PTSD symptoms.

As James continued his microdosing regimen, he experienced greater mental clarity and emotional stability. He was better equipped to manage his anxiety and face the traumatic memories that haunted him. Over time, he noticed improvements in his sleep, mood, and overall well-being.

James also began incorporating mindfulness practices, such as meditation and breathwork, into his daily routine. This combination of microdosing and mindfulness helped him cultivate a more balanced and compassionate perspective toward his past experiences.

After several months of microdosing, James felt renewed hope and purpose in his life. He reconnected with old friends, found a fulfilling job, and even started volunteering at a local community center. While he acknowledges that his journey is far from over, James credits microdosing magic mushrooms as a crucial catalyst for his healing and transformation.

Through his story, James demonstrates the potential of microdosing as a powerful tool in overcoming trauma and rebuilding a meaningful life after PTSD. His experience serves as a testament to the possibilities that alternative treatments can offer to those struggling with the aftermath of trauma.

Story 2: Macrodosing and Transformative Healing

Samantha, a 28-year-old survivor of childhood abuse, had been living with PTSD for most of her life. The trauma left her with chronic anxiety, depression, and a deep-rooted sense of unworthiness. Her symptoms persisted despite years of therapy and medication, and she felt stuck in her pain.

At the recommendation of her therapist, Samantha decided to explore the potential of macrodosing magic mushrooms for healing. She researched the process extensively and, with the help of a trained guide, embarked on a carefully planned and supervised journey.

During her macrodosing session, Samantha experienced a profound sense of interconnectedness with the world around her. She encountered vivid visions and powerful emotions that allowed her to confront her traumatic past from a new perspective. The experience was both challenging and cathartic, as she faced her fears and embraced the depth of her emotions.

In the following days and weeks, Samantha worked closely with her therapist to integrate the insights and revelations from her macrodosing experience. She began cultivating self-compassion and forgiveness for her younger self and started to see the strength and resilience she had developed from her past experiences.

As Samantha continued to process her macrodosing journey, she noticed a significant improvement in her mental health. Her anxiety and depression lessened, her relationships improved, and she felt more connected to herself and others.

Samantha's transformative healing through macrodosing magic mushrooms highlights the potential of this approach for addressing deep-rooted trauma. By facing her past in a supportive and therapeutic context, Samantha could break through barriers that had held her back for years and find a newfound sense of peace and wholeness.

Story 3: Enhanced Creativity and Emotional Resilience

Ethan, a 35-year-old artist, had struggled with the emotional aftermath of a traumatic event for years. His PTSD manifested as anxiety, creative blocks, and an inability to cope with stress. Ethan felt disconnected from his art and his own emotions, which left him feeling lost and unfulfilled.

After hearing about the benefits of microdosing magic mushrooms, Ethan decided to try it. He hoped that by incorporating microdosing into his daily routine, he could regain his creative spark and develop greater emotional resilience.

Over several months, Ethan followed a carefully designed microdosing protocol, taking small doses of magic mushrooms every few days. He noticed that as he continued his microdosing regimen, his creativity flowed more freely. He found himself producing new and inspired artwork, and his passion for his craft was reignited.

In addition to his creative breakthroughs, Ethan also experienced increased emotional resilience. He found himself better equipped to handle stress and anxiety and more capable of navigating difficult emotions when they arose. The microdosing regimen helped him cultivate a more profound sense of self-awareness and emotional intelligence, which allowed him to face his PTSD symptoms head-on and find healthier ways to cope.

Ethan's story showcases the potential of microdosing magic mushrooms for enhancing creativity and fostering emotional resilience. By incorporating this practice into his daily life, Ethan could reconnect with his art, better manage his PTSD symptoms, and experience a renewed sense of purpose and joy.

Story 4: A Holistic Approach to Treating PTSD

Samantha, a 42-year-old veteran, had been living with PTSD for years due to her time in the military. The traditional therapies she tried offered some relief, but she continued to struggle with nightmares, flashbacks, and emotional numbness. Samantha knew she needed to explore alternative treatments and decided to take a holistic approach to her healing journey.

She began researching the potential benefits of magic mushrooms for PTSD and decided to incorporate both microdosing and macrodosing into her treatment plan. In addition to using psychedelics, Samantha embraced a range of complementary therapies and practices, such as yoga, meditation, and breathwork, to support her mental and emotional well-being.

Over several months, Samantha followed a microdosing protocol, taking small doses of magic mushrooms every few days. She also participated in a few guided macrodosing sessions, which allowed her to confront and process the traumatic memories that haunted her. Through these experiences, she gained valuable insights and a greater understanding of her emotions.

The combination of psychedelic therapy and holistic practices profoundly impacted Samantha's healing journey. She found that the physical and mental benefits of yoga, meditation, and breathwork helped her stay grounded and present, making integrating the insights she gained from her magic mushroom experiences easier.

By embracing a holistic approach to treating PTSD, Samantha was able to alleviate her symptoms, develop a more profound sense of self-awareness, and ultimately achieve a more balanced and fulfilling life. Her story demonstrates the power of combining traditional and alternative therapies to create a personalized, comprehensive treatment plan that addresses the multifaceted nature of PTSD.

Story 5: Rebuilding Relationships and Trust through Magic Mushrooms

Tom, a 35-year-old first responder, had been struggling with PTSD for several years due to the traumatic events he had witnessed on the job. The condition significantly affected his personal life, as he found it increasingly difficult to connect with his loved ones and maintain healthy relationships.

As his relationships began to deteriorate, Tom sought help from various therapies and medications, but none seemed to have a lasting impact. Desperate for a solution, he explored the potential benefits of magic mushrooms for his PTSD.

Tom began by participating in a guided macrodosing session, during which he faced and processed some of the deeply rooted traumas that had been haunting him. The experience was intense and challenging but ultimately liberating, as he gained a new perspective on his past experiences and emotions.

After his macrodosing session, Tom continued his healing journey by incorporating microdosing into his daily routine. The combination of macrodosing and microdosing helped him to understand his emotions better and to develop a newfound sense of empathy and compassion, not just for himself but also for those around him.

As a result of his experiences with magic mushrooms, Tom found that he was better equipped to rebuild his relationships and reestablish trust with his loved ones. He discovered that the open, honest communication and vulnerability he had learned during his psychedelic journey translated into his personal life, allowing him to reconnect with his family and friends on a deeper level.

Tom's story highlights the potential of magic mushrooms to not only alleviate PTSD symptoms but also to foster personal growth and development. By incorporating psychedelic therapy into his healing process, Tom was able to improve not just his mental health but also his relationships, ultimately leading to a more fulfilling and connected life.

Story 6: Reclaiming Inner Peace through Nature and Magic Mushrooms

Samantha, a 28-year-old military veteran, had been struggling with PTSD since returning from her deployment overseas. The symptoms of her PTSD, including nightmares, anxiety, and emotional numbness, made it difficult for her to find joy and meaning in her daily life.

In search of a way to heal, Samantha came across the idea of using magic mushrooms to address her PTSD symptoms. Intrigued by the potential of this natural treatment, she decided to try it. Samantha combined her magic mushroom experiences with her love for nature to maximize her healing potential.

Samantha started with a guided macrodosing session in a secluded natural setting, which allowed her to confront and process the traumatic memories that had been haunting her. The immersive and supportive environment helped her feel safe and connected, making exploring her emotions and experiences easier.

Following the success of her macrodosing session, Samantha incorporated microdosing into her routine. She also made a point to spend more time in nature, using the healing power of the outdoors to complement her magic mushroom therapy.

Over time, Samantha noticed significant improvements in her mental health. Her anxiety began to subside, her nightmares became less frequent, and she started to experience a renewed sense of inner peace. By combining the therapeutic effects of magic mushrooms with nature's healing power, Samantha could reclaim control over her life and find a new sense of balance and wholeness.

Samantha's story demonstrates the potential of magic mushrooms to facilitate deep healing when combined with complementary practices, such as spending time in nature. This holistic approach allowed Samantha to address her PTSD symptoms and rediscover her passion for life, ultimately leading to a more fulfilling and peaceful existence.

Story 7: Building a Mindful Practice with Magic Mushrooms

Daniel, a 35-year-old emergency room nurse, had been struggling with the lingering effects of PTSD following a series of traumatic experiences at work. Despite seeking professional help, Daniel found it challenging to fully engage in traditional therapies, often feeling detached and disconnected from his emotions.

Daniel's search for alternative methods led him to magic mushrooms. He began researching their potential benefits for PTSD and discovered numerous accounts of positive experiences. Intrigued by the possibility of integrating magic mushrooms into his healing journey, he decided to try it.

Daniel started by incorporating microdosing into his daily routine, using small amounts of magic mushrooms to shift his perspective and improve his mood gently. He noticed that microdosing helped him feel more present and connected to his emotions, enabling him to engage more deeply in therapy sessions.

To further enhance his healing journey, Daniel also began practicing mindfulness meditation. He found that the combination of magic mushrooms and meditation allowed him to cultivate greater self-awareness, making it easier to process and release the traumas holding him back.

Over time, Daniel experienced significant improvements in his overall well-being. His PTSD symptoms, including flashbacks and hypervigilance, began to subside, and he developed a greater sense of inner peace and resilience.

Daniel's story highlights the potential of combining magic mushrooms with mindfulness practices to create a robust and holistic approach to healing from PTSD. By integrating these complementary modalities, Daniel could confront and process his traumas, ultimately finding a renewed sense of balance, wholeness, and emotional stability.

Story 8: Reclaiming Power and Breaking Barriers with Macrodosing

Linda, a 40-year-old firefighter, had been battling PTSD symptoms triggered by a near-death experience she had while on duty. She constantly feared that every time she responded to an emergency, it might be her last. This chronic stress affected her job performance, relationships, and mental health. Despite undergoing conventional treatments and therapies, Linda felt that she was merely surviving, not truly living.

Desperate for a breakthrough, Linda decided to try macrodosing magic mushrooms under the supervision of a qualified guide. During her session, she was taken on a journey that led her to confront her deepest fears and insecurities. At some point in the experience, she envisioned herself in a vast, open field, standing in front of a wall that symbolized her emotional and mental barriers.

With a newfound sense of empowerment, she "climbed" this wall in her vision, realizing that her limitations were self-imposed and she had the strength to overcome them. This experience, although metaphorical, had a profoundly transformative effect on Linda's psyche.

In the following days, Linda began working with a therapist to integrate and apply her experiences to her everyday life. She started practicing mindfulness techniques to help her manage stress and anxiety, and her fear of the job significantly diminished. Over time, Linda began to excel at work, and her relationships improved. She finally felt like she was reclaiming her life, and this newfound sense of power and purpose had a ripple effect, inspiring those around her to seek healing and transformation.

Linda's journey is a powerful illustration of the transformative potential of macrodosing magic mushrooms, particularly for those who have hit a roadblock in their conventional treatment for PTSD. Her experience redefined her understanding of strength and resilience, helping her to break free from the cycle of fear and anxiety that had imprisoned her for so long.

For More Information on Athletic Performance

If using magic mushrooms to improve athletic performance within PTSD recovery has piqued your interest, then there's a resource you won't want to overlook. The book 'The Athlete's Trip: Unleashing the Potential of Magic Mushrooms for Athletic Performance' is designed to deepen your understanding and provide actionable steps to achieve mental and physical gains. Take the next step toward holistic well-being by grabbing your copy today.

By sharing these individual stories of triumph over trauma through the use of magic mushrooms, we aim to inspire and provide practical insights for those navigating their paths of healing. Each story underscores the remarkable resilience of the human spirit and the vast potential of these alternative treatments in helping people reclaim their lives. Remember, while the journey may be your own, you are never alone.

Lessons Learned and Insights from Personal Journeys

The personal stories shared in this chapter reveal the diverse ways in which magic mushrooms can be utilized to support healing from PTSD. These accounts highlight the unique and transformative experiences of individuals who have courageously embarked on their journeys toward recovery. While each story is distinct, several key insights and lessons can be gleaned from these personal journeys:

Personalized approach: Each individual's path to healing is unique, and what works for one person may not necessarily work for another. It is essential to approach magic mushrooms with an open mind, experimenting with different dosages, schedules, and complementary practices to find the most effective and meaningful combination for your needs and circumstances.

The importance of set and setting: As demonstrated in these stories, paying attention to set and setting is crucial in facilitating a safe, supportive, and transformative experience with magic mushrooms. Cultivating a positive mindset, creating a comfortable environment, and surrounding oneself with supportive individuals can significantly impact the outcome of both microdosing and macrodosing sessions.

The value of integration: Many individuals in these stories emphasized the importance of integrating the insights and experiences gained from their work with magic mushrooms. This may involve journaling, creative expression, discussing experiences with a trusted friend or therapist, or practicing mindfulness techniques. Integration is key to ensuring that the benefits of magic mushrooms are sustained and incorporated into daily life.

The power of combining modalities: The stories also highlight the benefits of combining magic mushrooms with other therapeutic modalities and practices, such as therapy, meditation, breathwork, or yoga. By adopting a holistic approach and integrating various healing tools, individuals can maximize the therapeutic potential of magic mushrooms and create a more comprehensive and effective treatment plan.

Patience and perseverance: Healing from PTSD is a complex and often challenging process. The personal stories shared here serve as a reminder that patience and perseverance are essential in navigating the ups and downs of the healing journey. It is crucial to remember that progress may be gradual and nonlinear, but with dedication and self-compassion, lasting change is possible.

By examining these personal journeys, we gain valuable insights into the potential of magic mushrooms as a powerful tool for healing from PTSD. Each individual's experience offers a unique perspective on these entheogens' transformative potential and inspires those seeking alternative paths to recovery and personal growth.

Building a Holistic Healing Plan

Are you ready to amplify the healing potential of magic mushrooms in your journey to recover from PTSD? If so, you're in the right place. This chapter dives deep into creating a holistic healing plan that integrates the power of magic mushrooms with a range of other transformative practices and strategies. We'll reveal how the synergy between psilocybin and therapies like yoga, meditation, and community support can bring about profound, lasting change—far more significant than any single approach could achieve.

From discussing various therapeutic models to integrating mind-body practices such as yoga and meditation, we'll guide you through designing your comprehensive healing plan. We'll even delve into often-overlooked factors like nutrition and lifestyle, ensuring you have all the tools you need for a holistic recovery. By the end of this chapter, you'll understand how to personalize your approach for maximum effectiveness, embracing a path that not only addresses your PTSD symptoms but also fosters more profound emotional, mental, and physical well-being. Let's begin this transformative journey together.

The Importance of a Comprehensive Approach

When it comes to healing from PTSD, a one-size-fits-all approach just won't cut it. Post-Traumatic Stress Disorder is a complex condition with many symptoms that can manifest physically, emotionally, mentally, and spiritually. While the transformative experiences facilitated by magic mushrooms have proven to be a powerful catalyst for change, they are often most effective when part of a broader, more comprehensive treatment plan.

Imagine your healing journey as building a house. While magic mushrooms might serve as the robust cornerstone, the stability of the entire structure depends on other elements: the walls, the roof, and even the intricate wiring and plumbing inside. A comprehensive approach to your healing is akin to this well-built house, layered and interconnected, providing a resilient shelter against the storms of life.

Let's talk specifics. In a comprehensive approach, you're not just attacking the symptoms of PTSD; you're addressing root causes, many of which may be intertwined and multi-dimensional. This means looking at how diet and nutrition can affect mental health, or how mindfulness practices like yoga and meditation can enhance emotional regulation. It could involve complementary therapies such as Cognitive Behavioral Therapy (CBT), Eye Movement Desensitization and Reprocessing (EMDR), or Somatic Experiencing to integrate the psychological insights gained from magic mushroom sessions.

The benefits of such a well-rounded strategy extend beyond immediate symptom relief. As you engage in various therapies and practices, you develop a toolkit of coping mechanisms and skills that prepare you for the challenges of everyday life. Over time, these resources contribute to sustained resilience, emotional balance, and psychological well-being, allowing for a deeper and more lasting transformation.

A comprehensive approach also has the advantage of being highly adaptable. Since each person's experience with PTSD is unique, the best treatment plans can be tailored to individual needs, preferences, and lifestyles. Think of it as a personalized roadmap to recovery that you can adjust as you go, fine-tuning your path to healing and wholeness.

In summary, adopting a comprehensive approach to healing amplifies the effectiveness of each treatment, including magic mushrooms, providing a multi-faceted framework for overcoming PTSD. This strategy ensures that all aspects of your being are nurtured and supported, making it more likely to recover and thrive.

Therapeutic Models Incorporating Magic Mushrooms

In recent years, as the stigma surrounding psychedelics has dissipated, medical professionals and therapists increasingly acknowledge the substantial therapeutic potential of magic mushrooms. Consequently, various therapeutic models have been developed that amalgamate the transformative capabilities of these entheogens with established psychotherapeutic frameworks. The aim is to create a seamless, holistic experience that safely guides individuals through the complex terrain of their inner world, offering tools and techniques to process and integrate their newfound insights.

Psychedelic-assisted psychotherapy: This model has gained significant traction and scientific validation in recent years. It involves a structured program of multiple sessions, including preparatory meetings, the psychedelic journey, and post-experience integration. The prep sessions educate you on the effects and expectations while helping you establish an intention for the psychedelic experience. Therapists then accompany you through the psychedelic session, creating a safe space for exploration and emotional release. The post-journey integration sessions serve as crucial follow-ups, enabling you to interpret your experiences, metabolize the emotional material, and strategize ways to incorporate the insights into daily life.

Group therapy: While the psychedelic experience is deeply personal, sharing that journey within a trusted community can amplify its healing effects. This model combines individual psychedelic experiences with group sessions that allow participants to share their own stories, insights, and challenges, enhancing collective wisdom and empathic understanding. This shared narrative can be incredibly transformative for those whose PTSD symptoms involve feelings of isolation or detachment, offering a therapeutic milieu of support and communal resilience.

Mindfulness-based therapies: When synergized with mindfulness techniques like meditation or focused breathing, the healing potential of magic mushrooms can be significantly amplified. Such an approach encourages individuals to be fully present during their psychedelic experience, honing their ability to observe thoughts and feelings without judgment. The combination offers a unique pathway for cultivating a more harmonious relationship between the conscious and subconscious mind, providing an effective mechanism for navigating trauma.

Somatic therapies: Trauma is often stored in the body, not just the mind. Somatic approaches like yoga or specialized bodywork, provide an avenue for releasing these deeply entrenched physical memories. When combined with magic mushrooms, the resulting mind-body synthesis allows for a more integrative form of healing, addressing the energetic imbalances and chronic tension patterns that often accompany PTSD.

Cognitive Behavioral Therapy (CBT): This widely-used form of therapy focuses on identifying and changing negative thought patterns and behaviors. When used with magic mushrooms, CBT can help you understand the underlying thought patterns contributing to your PTSD symptoms, offering more focused opportunities for transformation during your psychedelic journeys.

Art Therapy: Utilizing creative expression as a form of emotional release can be particularly effective when combined with psychedelics. The intensified emotional awareness and diminished self-censorship often experienced during a magic mushroom session can provide rich material for artistic exploration, offering an alternative route for expressing and processing complex emotions.

Narrative Therapy: This therapy focuses on reshaping the narrative or story that individuals tell themselves about their lives and experiences. Magic mushrooms can serve as catalysts for seeing one's life from different perspectives, which can then be woven into a new, empowering narrative under the guidance of a skilled therapist.

Music Therapy: Music has a powerful effect on our emotions and can be a significant addition to the therapeutic process. Curated playlists can be created during the psychedelic experience to evoke specific emotional states or facilitate deep introspection.

Eco-Therapy or Nature Therapy: Some individuals find healing through a connection with nature. Using magic mushrooms in a natural setting, under a trained therapist's guidance, can enhance feelings of interconnectedness and reduce symptoms of PTSD related to disconnection or isolation.

Transpersonal Psychology: This approach incorporates spiritual, mystical, or altered states of consciousness into the therapeutic process. Given the often mystical or spiritual nature of magic mushroom experiences, transpersonal psychology can provide a framework for integrating such experiences into a broader understanding of oneself and one's place in the universe.

Attachment-Based Therapy: For those whose trauma has significantly impacted their ability to form healthy relationships, this therapy focuses on creating a secure therapist-client attachment as a 'corrective emotional experience.' When combined with magic mushrooms, the deep emotional insights can be directly applied to improve interpersonal relationships.

While each therapeutic model has unique advantages and limitations, many find that a fusion of multiple approaches yields the most transformative results. It is essential to consider these various models as a menu of options, each providing a unique flavor to your overall healing cuisine. By incorporating one or more into your personalized treatment plan, you'll be better positioned to fully leverage the profound healing capabilities of magic mushrooms on your path to recovery from PTSD.

Mind-Body Practices (Yoga, Meditation, Breathwork)

Incorporating mind-body practices can act as a powerful adjunct to the use of magic mushrooms in the quest to mitigate PTSD symptoms. These practices promote physical health and cultivate mental resilience, emotional intelligence, and spiritual growth. Each of these disciplines—yoga, meditation, and breathwork—offers distinct yet overlapping benefits that can enrich your healing journey synergistically when combined with psychedelic therapy.

Yoga: The Embodied Practice for Releasing Trauma
Yoga is not merely an exercise regime; it's an integrated system of holistic wellness rooted in ancient philosophy. It has the unique capability to address the physical, mental, emotional, and even spiritual aspects of our being. By combining postures, breath control, and meditation, yoga creates a multi-dimensional approach to well-being that can be particularly beneficial for those recovering from PTSD. When coupled with magic mushrooms' transformative power, yoga can become a cornerstone in a comprehensive healing plan.

Physical Benefits: Releasing Stored Tension

Yoga postures, known as asanas, help in releasing muscular tension. For individuals dealing with PTSD, this is vital. Trauma often manifests as physical tension or pain in the body. Specific asanas targeting areas like the hips and shoulders, where stress is commonly held, can help release these tension pockets. This physical relaxation can prepare your body to absorb the healing effects of magic mushrooms better, fostering a deeper level of recovery.

Mental Benefits: Mindfulness in Motion

Yoga requires concentration and mindfulness, teaching you to focus on your breath and sensations in your body as you flow through the postures. This awareness creates a 'mindfulness in motion,' allowing you to become more attuned to your mental and emotional state. Such mindfulness practices can amplify the insights gained during magic mushroom sessions by helping you become more receptive and conscious of your thoughts and feelings.

Emotional Benefits: Regulation and Resilience

Yoga has been shown to help regulate emotional responses by activating the parasympathetic nervous system, which calms the 'fight or flight' reaction often overactive in PTSD sufferers. The emotional balance that yoga brings can be a stabilizing force, making it easier to process the potentially overwhelming emotions that can arise during and after a psychedelic experience.

Spiritual Benefits: Cultivating Inner Peace

Beyond the physical and mental realms, yoga offers spiritual benefits. Whether or not you subscribe to a particular faith or spiritual belief, the practice encourages an inner journey toward peace and self-acceptance. The introspective nature of yoga complements the profound existential and spiritual insights that magic mushrooms can offer, creating a more holistic healing experience.

<u>Scientific Backing and Testimonials</u>
Numerous studies have underscored the benefits of yoga for trauma recovery, noting reductions in symptoms of depression, anxiety, and PTSD following a regular yoga practice. Personal accounts further echo these findings, as many individuals have reported experiencing a greater sense of peace, reduced PTSD symptoms, and enhanced self-awareness after integrating yoga into their healing regimen.

<u>Practical Tips: Getting Started</u>
If you're new to yoga, consider starting with a gentle form like Hatha or Restorative Yoga. As you become more comfortable, you may explore other styles and even specific postures that focus on opening and relaxing tension-prone areas of the body. Many online platforms and local studios offer classes specifically designed for stress and trauma recovery.

By weaving yoga into your holistic healing approach, alongside magic mushrooms and other therapeutic modalities, you can nurture your body, mind, and spirit in a profoundly transformative way.

Meditation: The Mindful Way to Inner Peace

Meditation is more than a method of relaxation; it's a discipline that offers profound mental transformation. When integrated into a holistic healing plan that includes magic mushrooms, meditation can be a potent ally in recovering from PTSD. Below, we explore how meditation complements various dimensions of well-being, making it an essential tool for those seeking mental clarity, emotional resilience, and lasting peace.

<u>Cognitive Benefits: Boosting Mental Clarity</u>
Meditation practices are designed to hone your attention and enhance your cognitive functioning. Over time, meditation can improve focus, boost memory retention, and facilitate

problem-solving abilities. These cognitive gains can be beneficial when trying to process and integrate the often complex and layered experiences elicited by magic mushrooms, providing the mental clarity required to turn insights into actionable change.

Emotional Benefits: Navigating Emotional Landscapes

One of the most immediate benefits of meditation is emotional regulation. PTSD often involves severe emotional fluctuations and distress. Meditation offers a structured space to become acquainted with these emotions without judgment. Techniques like mindfulness can help you objectively observe your emotional responses, making it easier to cope with stressors and triggers. The emotional self-mastery gained through meditation can be transformative, mainly when used in conjunction with the therapeutic benefits of magic mushrooms.

Psychological Benefits: Healing the Mind from Within

Numerous studies have indicated that meditation can substantially reduce symptoms related to anxiety, depression, and PTSD. The practice encourages disengagement from negative thought patterns and fosters a sense of internal peace. This psychological grounding can prove invaluable for those working through the mental and emotional challenges that accompany PTSD, offering a steadying mental foundation on which to build.

Spiritual Benefits: Connection and Oneness

While not overtly religious, meditation can be a profoundly spiritual experience, fostering a sense of interconnectedness and greater purpose. These spiritual dimensions can be heightened and explored further in the context of psychedelic experiences, where questions of existentialism often come to the fore. The sense of inner peace and connection gained through meditative practices can complement magic mushrooms' spiritual insights, enriching the healing journey.

<u>Scientific Backing: Evidence-Based Efficacy</u>
The benefits of meditation are not merely anecdotal; a growing body of scientific research supports them. Neuroimaging studies have shown structural changes in areas of the brain associated with attention, emotional regulation, and mental clarity following consistent meditation practice. The empirical data lends credibility to meditation as a valuable part of a comprehensive PTSD treatment plan.

<u>Practical Tips: Starting Your Meditation Journey</u>
If you're new to meditation, you should start with guided sessions, readily available online or through mobile apps. As you become more comfortable, you can explore different forms of meditation, such as mindfulness, transcendental, or loving-kindness, each offering unique benefits that can be tailored to your needs.

Integrating meditation into your holistic healing strategy, especially with the potent effects of magic mushrooms, can equip you with the mental and emotional skills necessary for lasting recovery from PTSD.

Breathwork: The Bridge Between Body and Mind
Breathwork is an evolving practice that extends far beyond simple deep breathing exercises. It is a dynamic form of active meditation, enabling you to deliberately regulate your physiological and emotional states. As part of a holistic healing plan for PTSD—especially when combined with magic mushrooms—breathwork can offer many benefits. Below are the various dimensions where breathwork can serve as a complementary therapy.

<u>Physiological Benefits: Regulating the Autonomic Nervous System</u>
Breathwork techniques often target the autonomic nervous system, which governs unconscious processes like heart rate,

digestion, and stress response. By consciously controlling your breath, you can influence this system, promoting relaxation and lowering stress hormones. This physiological regulation can be particularly helpful for individuals with PTSD, who often experience heightened arousal or stress.

Emotional Benefits: A Safe Release Valve
The emotional release facilitated by breathwork can be profound. Specific breathing techniques aim to unlock suppressed emotions, providing a safe and structured setting for their release. For individuals grappling with PTSD, this controlled emotional release can be a cathartic experience, beneficial after intense magic mushroom sessions where deep-rooted emotions may surface.

Psychological Benefits: Accessing Altered States
Breathwork allows you to access different levels of consciousness intentionally. For instance, techniques like Holotropic Breathwork are designed to induce states of consciousness that enable profound introspection and emotional release. These altered states can serve as a practice ground for the more intense shifts in consciousness facilitated by magic mushrooms, allowing for a smoother, more grounded psychedelic experience.

Enhancing Magic Mushroom Experiences: Synergistic Effects
When used with magic mushrooms, breathwork can potentiate the psychedelic experience. The controlled breathing patterns can help you dive deeper into your subconscious mind, making it easier to face and process trauma. Moreover, the grounding nature of breathwork can serve as an emotional anchor during the sometimes tumultuous psychedelic experiences, providing a sense of safety and control.

Spiritual Benefits: Cosmic Connectedness
Much like meditation, breathwork can also have spiritual implications. Many individuals report experiences of oneness or

interconnectedness during intense breathwork sessions, feelings that are often echoed during psychedelic experiences. This spiritual alignment can be crucial to holistic healing, imbuing the journey with a greater sense of purpose and meaning.

<u>Getting Started: Practical Steps</u>
Beginning your breathwork journey can be as simple as finding a quiet space and dedicating a few minutes daily to focused breathing. Various online resources and workshops offer guided sessions and tutorials to help you explore different breathwork techniques. As you become more adept, you may attend facilitated group sessions or one-on-one breathwork therapy to deepen your practice. By incorporating breathwork into your holistic healing strategy, particularly in tandem with magic mushroom therapy, you're likely to find a potent combination that aids in emotional regulation, alleviates physiological symptoms, and supports a lasting recovery from PTSD.

Embracing the synergistic blend of yoga, meditation, and breathwork in your healing journey amplifies the transformative potential of magic mushrooms in the treatment of PTSD. These mind-body practices serve as a unique pillar supporting your overall well-being—yoga for embodied physical release, meditation for mental clarity and emotional resilience, and breathwork as a bridge linking body and mind. When combined with the introspective and therapeutic properties of magic mushrooms, these practices form a comprehensive, evidence-informed approach to achieving long-lasting recovery. Together, they provide a robust framework for personal growth, profound self-discovery, and sustainable healing from the multifaceted challenges of PTSD.

Support Networks and Community

A strong support network and community are essential components of a holistic healing plan when using magic mushrooms to treat PTSD. The people around you can significantly impact your journey towards recovery, providing emotional support, understanding, and guidance. Building a network of trusted individuals and engaging with like-minded communities can enhance your healing process and contribute to lasting change.

Family and friends: Your close family members and friends can provide a strong foundation for your support network. Share your experiences and goals with them, and involve them in your healing process. Having loved ones who understand your journey can be invaluable in times of need, offering comfort, reassurance, and encouragement.

Therapists and professionals: Collaborating with mental health professionals, such as therapists and counselors, can be crucial in navigating the complexities of PTSD treatment. These professionals can help you process your experiences with magic mushrooms, provide guidance on integrating insights, and assist in developing coping strategies to manage PTSD symptoms.

Support groups: In person or online, joining support groups can connect you with others who share similar experiences and goals. These groups provide a safe space to discuss your journey, exchange information, and learn from one another. Engaging with support groups can foster a sense of belonging, reduce feelings of isolation, and create opportunities for personal growth.

Entheogenic communities: Entheogenic communities are individuals interested in using psychedelics for healing and personal growth. These communities can be found online and offline and provide valuable resources, education, and support for those using magic mushrooms as part of their healing process.

Workshops, retreats, and training programs: Participating in workshops, retreats, or training programs focused on magic mushrooms, PTSD, or related healing practices can deepen your understanding and strengthen your connection with others on similar journeys. These events often provide immersive experiences, access to experts, and opportunities for personal growth.

Cultivating a solid support network and engaging with communities that share your goals is vital in building a holistic healing plan. These connections can provide you with the resources, encouragement, and guidance necessary to navigate the challenges of PTSD treatment and create lasting change.

Nutrition and Lifestyle Changes

In addition to incorporating magic mushrooms into your healing journey, making targeted nutrition and lifestyle changes can significantly support your overall mental and emotional well-being. These changes can help you create a solid foundation for healing from PTSD and maximize the benefits of your psychedelic experiences.

Balanced diet: A well-balanced diet that includes a variety of whole, nutrient-dense foods can positively impact mental health. Consuming plenty of fruits, vegetables, organic whole grains, protein, and healthy fats can provide essential nutrients that support brain function and emotional resilience.

Hydration: Staying adequately hydrated is crucial for overall mental health. Dehydration can negatively affect mood, cognition, and energy levels. Aim to drink adequate amounts of clean, fluoride-free water daily to maintain optimal hydration.

Exercise: Regular physical activity has been shown to reduce symptoms of anxiety and depression, improve mood, and increase resilience to stress. Incorporate a mix of aerobic, strength, and flexibility exercises into your routine to support physical and mental well-being.

Sleep: Prioritize sleep as an essential component of your healing journey. Poor sleep quality can exacerbate PTSD symptoms and hinder your progress. Establish a consistent sleep schedule and create a relaxing bedtime routine to promote restful and restorative sleep.

Stress management: Developing effective stress management techniques, such as mindfulness practices, deep breathing exercises, or progressive muscle relaxation, can help you navigate the challenges of PTSD treatment more effectively.

Limiting stimulants and depressants: Minimize the consumption of substances that can negatively impact mental health, such as excessive caffeine, alcohol, or nicotine. These substances can interfere with sleep, increase anxiety, and hinder your progress in healing from PTSD.

Social connections: Nurture meaningful relationships with friends, family, and community members. Engaging in social activities and connecting with others can improve mood, reduce feelings of isolation, and contribute to overall mental health.

By adopting these nutrition and lifestyle changes, you can create a supportive environment that enhances your healing process and complements the effects of magic mushrooms in treating PTSD. These changes can help you build a strong foundation for long-lasting recovery and personal growth.

Personalizing Your Plan for Optimal Results

When creating a holistic healing plan that incorporates magic mushrooms and complementary practices, it's essential to recognize that everyone's journey is unique. Personalizing your plan for optimal results involves considering your needs, preferences, and circumstances. Here are some suggestions for tailoring your healing plan to suit your unique situation best:

Self-assessment: Begin by reflecting on your needs, goals, and challenges concerning your PTSD symptoms. Consider what aspects of your life may require additional support or change, and prioritize these areas in your healing plan.

Consult professionals: Work with mental health professionals, such as therapists or counselors, knowledgeable about PTSD and psychedelic-assisted therapies. They can help you develop a tailored plan addressing your needs and goals.

Integrate various approaches: Select complementary practices that resonate with you and align with your goals. This may include mind-body practices, nutrition and lifestyle changes, support networks, and community involvement. Experiment with different approaches and techniques to find what works best for you.

Adapt to your needs: Be flexible and open to adjusting your plan as you progress your healing journey. Your needs and preferences may evolve, so it's essential to remain open to change and adaptation.

Monitor progress: Regularly evaluate your progress and note any changes in your PTSD symptoms, emotional well-being, or overall quality of life. This will help you identify what aspects of your plan work well and which areas may require further adjustments.

Practice patience and self-compassion: Healing from PTSD can be complex and lengthy. Remember to be patient with yourself and practice self-compassion as you navigate your healing journey. Acknowledge your successes and growth, and be gentle with yourself during difficult moments.

By personalizing your holistic healing plan, you can optimize the benefits of magic mushrooms and complementary practices in addressing your PTSD symptoms. This tailored approach will empower you to take charge of your healing process and support your journey toward lasting recovery and personal growth.

Navigating Challenges and Embracing Growth

Embarking on a healing journey with magic mushrooms for PTSD treatment can be a transformative experience, filled with moments of profound insight and personal growth. However, like any path toward healing, it can also come with challenges, setbacks, and periods of self-doubt. This chapter will explore strategies for navigating these difficulties and embracing growth throughout your journey.

By cultivating a growth mindset and self-compassion, learning to measure progress and success, addressing potential challenges and setbacks, and adapting and personalizing your healing journey, you can develop resilience and maintain momentum in your recovery process. This chapter will provide the tools and insights necessary to face these challenges with grace and perseverance, allowing you to continue moving towards a healthier and more fulfilling life.

Cultivating a Growth Mindset and Self-Compassion

An essential aspect of navigating challenges and embracing growth in your healing journey is cultivating a growth mindset and practicing self-compassion. A growth mindset is the belief that your abilities, intelligence, and emotional resilience can be developed and improved through dedication and effort. Embracing a growth mindset allows you to view challenges as growth opportunities rather than insurmountable obstacles.

Cultivating a growth mindset is pivotal not just in overcoming the obstacles and traumas that come with PTSD, but also in enhancing your general well-being and potential for personal transformation. A growth mindset is founded on the belief that abilities and intelligence can be developed, opening the door for continuous growth and learning.

First and foremost, it's essential to recognize and challenge your limiting beliefs. We all have internal narratives that dictate how we perceive ourselves and our capabilities. These negative thought patterns can become significant roadblocks to recovery and growth, whether it's a fear of failure, self-doubt, or self-sabotage. Tackling these limiting beliefs head-on involves acknowledging their existence and consciously deciding to replace them with positive affirmations and more constructive narratives. Understanding that personal growth often emerges from facing challenges and learning from mistakes can empower you to reframe these limiting beliefs as opportunities for progress.

Another integral component of a growth mindset is embracing the learning process as an ongoing, lifelong journey. The landscape of your inner life is ever-changing, and there's always something new to learn about yourself or the world around you. Nourish your curiosity by being open to new skills, strategies, and insights. This could range from diving into a book about cognitive-behavioral techniques to engaging in workshops that teach coping mechanisms for stress. Being open to new experiences and perspectives keeps the learning process vibrant and enriching, adding new tools to your wellness toolkit.

It's equally important to celebrate your small victories along the way. No matter how seemingly insignificant, each step is a building block towards your larger goals. Whether it's maintaining a consistent meditation routine for a week or finally confronting a trigger without feeling overwhelmed, these moments deserve recognition. Celebrating them boosts your self-esteem and reinforces the belief that you are capable of growth and change. This, in turn, fosters resilience and helps you maintain momentum.

Lastly, take into account the virtues of persistence and patience. Adopting a growth mindset doesn't mean you'll be free from challenges, setbacks, or failures. What it does mean is that you have the mental resilience to keep moving forward, even when the going gets tough. Personal growth and healing are not linear processes; they take time, effort, and patience. When faced with setbacks, remind yourself that each moment is a new opportunity for growth and that progress is still progress, no matter how slow it may seem.

Together, these strategies help you to forge a mindset geared towards ongoing development, better equipping you to navigate the complexities of PTSD recovery and the unpredictable nature of life itself.

In addition to cultivating a growth mindset, practicing self-compassion is vital for navigating the challenges of your healing journey. Self-compassion involves treating yourself with kindness, understanding, and empathy, especially during challenging moments. While a growth mindset equips you with the resilience and curiosity for ongoing self-improvement, self-compassion provides the emotional cushion and psychological space you need to deal with setbacks and challenges compassionately.

Start by acknowledging your emotions, in all their complexity and nuance. So often, we suppress feelings of pain, fear, or sadness, thinking that acknowledging them is a sign of weakness. However, these emotions are a natural response to your challenges and traumas. Permit yourself to feel them fully. Accepting your feelings without judgment or criticism is the first step in understanding what you need to heal.

Equally important is the practice of self-kindness, an aspect of self-compassion that's often neglected. Consider how you would speak to a close friend or loved one going through a tough time. You'd offer words of encouragement, kindness, and understanding. Now, turn that compassionate lens towards yourself. Internalize the knowledge that everyone has shortcomings, makes mistakes, and faces challenges—it's part of being human. By treating yourself with the same care and understanding, you're not excusing your mistakes or challenges but allowing yourself the emotional space to learn and grow from them.

Mindfulness, another cornerstone of self-compassion, offers a host of benefits. Engaging in mindfulness practices like meditation or deep breathing exercises helps anchor yourself in the present moment. Mindfulness can act as an emotional stabilizer, allowing you to observe your thoughts and feelings more detachedly, which can be incredibly useful in preventing emotional overwhelm. You become aware of what you're going through and better equipped to navigate your emotional landscape without being consumed by it.

Combining these elements—acknowledging your emotions, practicing self-kindness, and cultivating mindfulness—creates a solid foundation for a growth mindset and self-compassion. As you work through the challenges and obstacles on your path to recovery, these practices equip you with the emotional and psychological tools needed for genuine, lasting healing. They serve as invaluable allies in overcoming the hurdles that come with treating PTSD and in embracing the personal growth that arises from successfully navigating these challenges.

Measuring Progress and Success

As you progress through your healing journey with magic mushrooms and other complementary practices, evaluating your progress and celebrating your successes is essential. Measuring progress can help you stay motivated and recognize the positive changes in your life, whether subtle or gradual. Here are some strategies for tracking your progress and success:

Establish clear goals: Set specific, measurable, achievable, relevant, and time-bound (SMART) goals for your healing journey. These goals might include reducing the severity of PTSD symptoms, improving sleep quality, or fostering healthier relationships.

Track your experiences: Keep a journal or use a tracking app to document your adventures with microdosing, macrodosing, and other healing practices. Note any changes in your mood, energy levels, sleep patterns, and overall well-being.

Reflect on personal growth: Review your journal entries or tracking data to identify patterns and trends in your experiences. Reflect on the development and changes you've noticed in your PTSD symptoms and other areas of your life.

Seek feedback from others: Consult with trusted friends, family members, or mental health professionals to gain insights into the progress they've observed in your life. Their perspectives can provide valuable information and help you recognize changes you may not have noticed.

Adjust your goals as needed: Your plans may change or evolve as you progress in your healing journey. Be open to reassessing and refining your objectives to align with your current needs and aspirations.

Focus on holistic well-being: Remember that healing from PTSD is a multifaceted process encompassing emotional, psychological, physical, and spiritual dimensions. Celebrate your progress in all areas of your well-being, even if some aspects take longer.

Embrace non-linear progress: Understand that healing is often a non-linear process with ups and downs. Be patient with yourself and acknowledge that setbacks are a natural part of the journey. Use these experiences to learn and grow, and continue to move forward.

By measuring your progress and success, you'll be better equipped to stay motivated and committed to your healing journey. Acknowledging and celebrating your achievements can also foster a greater sense of self-worth and confidence in overcoming challenges and growing.

Addressing Potential Challenges and Setbacks

As you embark on your healing journey with magic mushrooms and complementary practices, it's crucial to recognize that challenges and setbacks are natural and to be expected. The key to success lies in your ability to navigate these obstacles effectively and use them as opportunities for growth. Here are some strategies to help you address potential challenges and setbacks:

Cultivate self-compassion: Be gentle with yourself when you encounter setbacks or difficulties. Recognize that healing is a complex process, and it's expected to experience ups and downs. Treat yourself with kindness and understanding, just as you would a loved one facing similar challenges.

Develop a support network: Surround yourself with people who understand your healing journey and can provide encouragement, empathy, and guidance. This may include friends, family members, support groups, or mental health professionals experienced in working with PTSD and psychedelic-assisted therapy.

Be flexible and adaptable: Recognize that your healing path may not unfold precisely as planned. Be open to adjusting your approach, incorporating new practices, or seeking additional support. Embrace the idea of continuous learning and growth.

Analyze and learn from setbacks: When you encounter challenges, take the time to reflect on the situation and identify any lessons or insights that can be gained. Use this information to inform your future actions and make positive changes in your healing journey.

Practice patience: Healing from PTSD and other traumas takes time, and progress may be slow or gradual. Remember to be patient with yourself and to trust in the process, even when it feels challenging or frustrating.

Maintain a growth mindset: Focus on cultivating a growth mindset, emphasizing that dedication and hard work can develop your abilities and potential. This perspective can help you view setbacks as opportunities for learning and growth, rather than permanent failures.

Stay committed to your goals: Despite challenges and setbacks, stay focused on your objectives and why you embarked on this healing journey. Keep your goals in mind, and remind yourself of the progress you've made thus far.

By preparing for and addressing potential challenges and setbacks, you can build resilience and develop the skills necessary to navigate your healing journey's inevitable ups and downs. This will help you stay committed to your path and empower you to continue moving forward, even in adversity.

Adapting and Personalizing Your Healing Journey

Each person's healing journey is unique, and finding the most effective path to address PTSD symptoms and promote personal growth requires adapting and personalizing your approach. You can optimize your chances of success and lasting change by tailoring your plan to your specific needs, preferences, and circumstances. Here are some tips for adapting and personalizing your healing journey:

Reflect on your needs: Consider your unique history, experiences, strengths, and challenges. What aspects of your life would benefit most from healing and growth? Identify your personal goals and priorities, and use them to guide your healing journey.

Experiment with different practices: Since every individual responds differently to various healing modalities, explore other methods to find what resonates best with you. This may include experimenting with different dosing protocols for magic mushrooms, trying various mind-body practices, or seeking out different types of therapy.

Monitor your progress and adjust as needed: Regularly assess your progress, and be prepared to adapt your plan based on your experiences and results. If something needs fixing, be open to trying new approaches or refining your current strategies.

Seek professional guidance: Work with mental health professionals, such as therapists or counselors, experienced in PTSD and psychedelic-assisted therapy. They can provide personalized advice, support, and recommendations based on your unique needs and circumstances.

Listen to your intuition: Trust your inner wisdom and listen to your intuition as you navigate your healing journey. If something doesn't feel right, honor that feeling and be open to exploring alternative paths.

Build a personalized support network: Surround yourself with people who understand and support your healing journey. This may include friends, family members, support groups, or mental health professionals. A strong support network can help you stay motivated and provide valuable insights as you adapt and personalize your plan.

Embrace your uniqueness: Remember that your healing journey is personal and unique. What works for others may not work for you, and vice versa. Honor your individuality and embrace the idea that there is no one-size-fits-all solution.

By adapting and personalizing your healing journey, you can create a plan uniquely suited to your needs, preferences, and goals. This will empower you to take charge of your recovery and foster lasting change and growth as you work towards healing from PTSD and other traumas.

Conclusion

As we draw this book to a close, our heartfelt aspiration is that you have not merely encountered information but have embarked on a transformative educational journey about the groundbreaking potential of magic mushrooms in treating PTSD. We've delved into the rich history and rigorous science underpinning these potent fungi and navigated the labyrinth of their therapeutic applications. We have aimed to craft a nuanced, all-encompassing guide, enriched by personal anecdotes, pragmatic advice, and resourceful insights to shepherd you through the multifaceted realm of psychedelic therapy tailored explicitly for PTSD.

It is vital, however, to underscore that this book is not an end but a significant milestone on your ongoing voyage toward healing and self-realization. Your path to recovery and growth is inherently personal ever-evolving, and necessitates an unwavering commitment to learning, adapting, and expanding your horizons. We urge you to remain a lifelong student in this evolving field, to connect with supportive and like-minded communities, and to continually refine your therapeutic strategies to make your healing process as impactful and life-affirming as possible.

As you may anticipate, the frontier of psychedelic research constantly pushes its boundaries, promising new revelations, sophisticated best practices, and revolutionary methodologies. By remaining engaged and updated, you position yourself at the forefront of this evolution—ready to make discerning, evidence-based decisions and to become a strong advocate for the responsible and compassionate use of magic mushrooms in treating PTSD.

Let this book act not just as a knowledge repository but as a kindling spark that ignites your journey toward healing. May it serve as both a wellspring of inspiration and a resolute testament to the transformative capabilities of magic mushrooms. Your path is your own, yet know you are supported by cumulative wisdom and hopeful advances in this field. Here's to your journey toward healing, growth, and the awe-inspiring process of self-discovery.

Before we part ways, let's revisit some key takeaways from our exploration together. Firstly, PTSD is a complex mental health condition with diverse symptoms and impacts, requiring equally nuanced and flexible treatment options. Magic mushrooms, rich in the psychoactive compound psilocybin, offer an alternative or complementary pathway to traditional treatments. They have shown significant potential in alleviating the symptoms of PTSD through various mechanisms, including enhanced neuroplasticity, improved emotional processing, and transformative mystical experiences.

Secondly, there are two main consumption methods for magic mushrooms in treating PTSD—microdosing and macrodosing. Each has its benefits and challenges, and choosing between them often boils down to your personal needs, comfort levels, and therapeutic goals. Microdosing involves taking sub-perceptual doses to effect subtle changes in mood and cognition, while macrodosing provides a more profound, immersive psychedelic experience designed for deeper healing.

Thirdly, the science and legality surrounding the use of magic mushrooms are rapidly evolving. Staying updated on the latest research and legal statutes ensures that you're well-informed and helps you advocate for responsible and ethical use.

Lastly, the journey toward healing is profoundly personal and ongoing. It requires a holistic approach, integrating both psychedelic experiences and traditional therapeutic practices. Magic mushrooms can be a tool in your toolkit but are not a silver bullet. Active participation in your healing journey—coupled with the support of healthcare professionals, community, and self-care practices—determines your recovery's overall success and sustainability.

With these key takeaways in mind, you are better positioned to navigate the intricate landscape of PTSD treatment options, always grounded in the latest science, personal introspection, and an unwavering commitment to your well-being.

The Future of Magic Mushrooms in PTSD Treatment

As we gaze toward the horizon, the future landscape of magic mushrooms as an innovative treatment modality for PTSD shines with unbounded potential and optimism. Bolstered by a surge in scientific inquiry, our evolving understanding of these potent psychedelics sheds invaluable light on their intricate mechanisms of action, efficacy, and safety profiles. Such expanding vistas of knowledge are poised to usher in an era of refined therapeutic protocols, democratized patient access, and mainstream acceptance of magic mushrooms as an indispensable asset in our mental health toolkit.

One fascinating frontier lies in the realm of bioengineering and pharmacology. Cutting-edge research explores the synthesis of novel compounds inspired by the active ingredient, psilocybin. These new molecular derivatives could offer tailored therapeutic benefits, while minimizing undesirable side effects, thereby revolutionizing the personalized treatment of PTSD.

Rigorously designed and ethically conducted clinical studies are paving the way for possible FDA approval of psilocybin-assisted therapy as a clinically recognized regimen for treating PTSD. Such approval would validate the efficacy of this form of treatment and extend the scope of insurance coverage, facilitating its integration into conventional healthcare infrastructures.

In parallel, the burgeoning interest in psychedelic therapies has catalyzed the formation of specialized training academies and professional guilds dedicated to setting benchmarks for ethical and responsible practices. As the number of practitioners skilled in psychedelic-assisted treatment swells, we can anticipate an enriched therapeutic landscape marked by enhanced quality, availability, and geographical spread of care.

Last but certainly not least, legislative shifts towards the decriminalization or even legalization of magic mushrooms are in progress across various global jurisdictions. These socio-political changes promise to significantly widen the door for individuals with PTSD to access this invaluable therapy. Coupled with a cultural paradigm shift towards viewing psychedelics through a lens of scientific evidence rather than stigmatization, these legal efforts will undoubtedly serve to mainstream and normalize the use of magic mushrooms in mental healthcare.

In sum, the future of magic mushrooms in treating PTSD is not just promising—it's electrifying. A mosaic of innovation, research breakthroughs, and evolving societal perspectives is painting a vivid tapestry of opportunities for therapeutic intervention. As we continue to unlock the multidimensional healing potential of these enigmatic fungi, we are simultaneously offering renewed hope and novel pathways for individuals grappling with PTSD not just to reclaim, but to transform their lives truly.

Personal Empowerment and Healing

Embarking on the journey to heal from PTSD is not merely an endeavor for recovery; it's a transformative odyssey that places you at the helm of your life's narrative. The use of magic mushrooms transcends the confines of conventional therapies, offering individuals a profound, active agency in scripting their tale of resurgence. This form of psychedelic therapy provides an unparalleled lens through which to view, interpret, and ultimately reshape the stories of trauma, emotional patterns, and interpersonal dynamics that have imprinted upon the soul.

Infusing magic mushrooms into a well-rounded therapeutic strategy, synergistically combined with talk therapy, mindfulness practices, and diligent self-care, provides an unprecedented opportunity to delve into the deep-seated roots of traumatic experiences. This integrative and holistic methodology is not just a comforting for symptoms but a potent catalyst for re-engineering emotional resilience, self-understanding, and an enduring sense of well-being.

The ripples of this personal metamorphosis extend far beyond the individual's inner world; they touch the lives of family members, friends, and acquaintances. Your renewed spirit and mental fortitude can become a beacon of hope and inspiration for others. As you reclaim agency and vitality, you unconsciously permit others to seek their paths of healing and understanding, thus nurturing a collective culture of compassion, empathy, and human connection.

Ultimately, magic mushrooms' role in treating PTSD is not just therapeutic—it's emancipatory. As you take charge of your healing journey, you're not just combating the symptoms of a disorder; you're reshaping your destiny. You're overcoming the haunting shadows of past trauma, laying the foundation for healthier relationships, and stitching together a vivid tapestry of a more harmonious, purposeful life.

In the grand scheme, the magic mushroom-assisted path to healing from PTSD serves as an invitation—to rise above the debilitating tentacles of trauma, forge enriching human connections and set forth into a brighter, more hopeful tomorrow, both for oneself and the larger tapestry of human interconnectedness to which we all belong.

Invitation to Share Experiences and Join the Community

As we conclude this exploration of magic mushrooms and their potential role in PTSD treatment, we invite you to share your experiences and insights with others on a similar journey. By opening up about your challenges and triumphs, you can contribute to a supportive and compassionate community of individuals working towards healing and personal growth.

There are various ways to connect with others who share your interest in using magic mushrooms for PTSD treatment. Online forums, social media groups, workshops, and retreats offer valuable learning opportunities, growth, and connections. By engaging with these communities, you can benefit from the collective wisdom and experiences of others while providing your unique perspective and support.

Sharing your story not only helps to normalize the conversation around magic mushrooms and PTSD treatment but also creates an environment in which others feel safe to share their own experiences. Together, we can raise awareness about the potential benefits of this powerful therapeutic tool, advocate for further research and accessibility, and promote the healing and transformation of countless individuals affected by trauma.

We encourage you to join this vibrant community by participating in online discussions, attending a local workshop, or simply sharing your experiences with friends and loved ones. By doing so, you can help to create a world in which the healing potential of magic mushrooms is recognized, embraced, and accessible to all who can benefit from its transformative power.

Frequently Asked Questions

As you explore the potential of magic mushrooms for treating PTSD, it's natural to have questions and concerns. In this chapter, we aim to address some of the most frequently asked questions about using magic mushrooms in the context of PTSD treatment. We'll provide insights and information on determining whether magic mushrooms are right for you, understanding potential side effects, finding a knowledgeable therapist, evaluating treatment progress, and considering possible risks and contraindications. By offering clear and concise answers to these common questions, we hope to empower you with the knowledge you need to make informed decisions about your healing journey.

How do I know if magic mushrooms are right for me?

Determining whether magic mushrooms are a suitable treatment option for your PTSD requires careful consideration of several factors. While many individuals have found relief from their symptoms through magic mushrooms, it's important to remember that each person's experience and needs are unique. Here are some factors to consider when deciding if magic mushrooms are right for you.

Personal history and health: Assess your mental and physical health and any history of substance use or addiction. If you have a personal or family history of schizophrenia, bipolar disorder, or other severe mental illnesses, using magic mushrooms may not be advisable. Consult with a mental health professional or a medical doctor to discuss concerns or potential risks.

Medications: If you take any drugs, particularly SSRIs or other psychiatric medications, consult a healthcare professional before considering magic mushrooms. Some medicines may interact negatively with psilocybin or reduce its effectiveness.

Emotional readiness: Having a solid emotional foundation and willingness to face and process difficult emotions or memories that may arise during the psychedelic experience is crucial. Reflect on your current emotional state and readiness to engage in this form of therapy.

Support network: Having a support system, such as friends, family, or a therapist familiar with psychedelic-assisted therapy, can be invaluable in guiding you through the healing process.

Legal considerations: Familiarize yourself with the legal status of magic mushrooms in your area, as possessing psilocybin-containing mushrooms is still illegal in many countries and jurisdictions.

Intuition and personal values: Ultimately, the decision to use magic mushrooms for PTSD treatment is deeply personal. Reflect on your values, beliefs, and intuition when considering whether this therapeutic approach aligns with your needs and preferences.

By considering these factors, you can make a more informed decision about whether magic mushrooms may be a suitable option for your PTSD treatment journey. Consult a qualified healthcare professional to discuss your specific circumstances and potential treatment options.

What are the potential side effects of microdosing and macrodosing?

Both microdosing and macrodosing with magic mushrooms can be associated with various side effects, although the intensity and frequency of these effects may differ between the two approaches. Awareness of these potential side effects is essential to ensure a safe and comfortable experience.

Microdosing side effects:

1. Physical: Some individuals may experience mild physical side effects such as headaches, nausea, or increased heart rate. These effects are usually short-lived and dissipate as the body adjusts to the microdose.
2. Emotional: Changes in mood, anxiety, or irritability may occur, although these are typically less pronounced than with macrodosing.
3. Cognitive: Some users report difficulty concentrating, short-term memory issues, or feeling "scattered" while microdosing.

Macrodosing side effects:

1. Physical: Macrodosing can cause more pronounced physical side effects such as nausea, vomiting, dizziness, increased heart rate, and changes in blood pressure. These effects are generally temporary and subside as the psychedelic experience comes to an end.
2. Emotional: Intense emotions, mood swings, and heightened anxiety can occur during a macrodosing session. Some individuals may also experience challenging or frightening experiences, known as "bad trips," which can be emotionally distressing.

3. Cognitive: Visual and auditory hallucinations, confusion, disorientation, and time distortion are common side effects of macrodosing.
4. After-effects: In the days following a macrodosing session, some individuals may experience a "psychedelic hangover," characterized by feelings of fatigue, brain fog, or emotional sensitivity.

It's essential to be aware of these potential side effects and to take necessary precautions to minimize risks, such as starting with a low dose, ensuring a proper set and setting, and having a trusted sitter or guide present during a macrodosing session. If you have pre-existing medical conditions or are taking medications, consult a healthcare professional before using magic mushrooms to discuss potential risks and contraindications.

How do I find a knowledgeable and supportive therapist?

Finding a knowledgeable and supportive therapist experienced in magic mushrooms and psychedelic-assisted therapy is crucial for a safe and effective healing journey. Here are some steps to help you find the right therapist.

Research: Start by learning about the different types of therapy and therapeutic approaches that incorporate magic mushrooms, such as psychedelic-assisted therapy, integration therapy, or harm reduction. This will help you determine which approach best suits your needs and preferences.

Online resources: Utilize online resources such as the Multidisciplinary Association for Psychedelic Studies (MAPS) or the Psychedelic Support network to find a list of trained therapists and practitioners in your area. These directories often include professionals with expertise in psychedelic-assisted therapy and integration.

Referrals: Ask for recommendations from friends, support groups, or online forums focused on psychedelic therapy. People with firsthand experience can provide valuable insights into the therapists they've worked with and their overall satisfaction with the process.

Interviews and consultations: Once you have identified potential therapists, schedule initial talks or discussions with each. This will allow you to discuss your needs, goals, and concerns and assess their expertise and experience with magic mushrooms.

Assess compatibility: It's essential to feel comfortable and supported by your therapist. Evaluate your level of rapport with each therapist and consider their communication style, empathy, and understanding of your unique circumstances.

Credentials and training: Verify the therapist's credentials, including their education, licensure, and any specialized training in psychedelic-assisted therapy or integration.

Informed consent and ethical considerations: Ensure the therapist you choose adheres to ethical guidelines and provides explicit, informed consent about the potential risks and benefits of using magic mushrooms in a therapeutic context.

By taking the time to research and evaluate potential therapists thoroughly, you can find a knowledgeable and supportive professional who will guide you through your healing journey with magic mushrooms.

How long does it take to see results from microdosing or macrodosing?

The timeline for experiencing results from microdosing or macrodosing magic mushrooms can vary significantly from person to person. Several factors, such as individual physiology, the severity of PTSD symptoms, and the chosen dosing protocol, can influence how quickly one notices changes.

For microdosing, some individuals report noticing subtle improvements in mood, focus, and overall well-being within a few days to a week of starting their regimen. However, it is more common for noticeable changes to emerge after several weeks or even months of consistent microdosing. Maintaining a regular schedule and following a proper microdosing protocol is essential to optimize the potential benefits.

In the case of macrodosing, the effects can be more immediate and profound. Some individuals may experience significant shifts in perspective, emotional processing, or symptom reduction after just one or a few high-dose sessions. However, it is crucial to remember that integrating these experiences into daily life is vital to the healing process. The lasting impact of macrodosing is often tied to the work done during the integration period, which can span weeks, months, or even longer.

Ultimately, the timeline for seeing results will depend on the individual's unique circumstances and commitment to working through the therapeutic process. Being patient and maintaining realistic expectations is essential, as healing from PTSD can be a gradual and nonlinear journey.

Can I combine magic mushrooms with other treatments or medications?

Combining magic mushrooms with other treatments or medications can be complex and requires careful consideration. There may be potential benefits to using a combination of therapies, but it is crucial to be aware of the risks and consult a knowledgeable healthcare professional before proceeding.

When combining magic mushrooms with other treatments, such as psychotherapy, meditation, or mind-body practices, there is often a synergistic effect that can enhance the overall healing process. These complementary therapies can help provide a more holistic approach to treating PTSD and address various mental and emotional well-being aspects.

However, when it comes to medications, the situation becomes more complicated. Combining magic mushrooms with certain medicines may lead to adverse effects or diminished efficacy. For example, combining psilocybin with selective serotonin reuptake inhibitors (SSRIs) or other psychiatric medications can result in unpredictable outcomes, such as reduced efficacy of the psilocybin or an increased risk of serotonin syndrome.

It is essential to consult with a knowledgeable healthcare professional or therapist familiar with magic mushrooms and your specific medication regimen. They can help assess the potential risks and benefits and guide you in making informed decisions about incorporating magic mushrooms into your treatment plan. Always prioritize your safety and well-being when combining magic mushrooms with other treatments or medications.

Are there any potential risks or contraindications to be aware of?

While magic mushrooms can be a powerful therapeutic tool for treating PTSD and fostering personal growth, it is essential to be aware of potential risks and contraindications to ensure a safe and beneficial experience.

Pre-existing mental health conditions: Individuals with a personal or family history of schizophrenia, bipolar disorder, or other severe psychiatric conditions should approach the use of magic mushrooms with caution. Psilocybin can potentially exacerbate symptoms or trigger the onset of these conditions in susceptible individuals.

Heart conditions: Magic mushrooms can cause an increase in heart rate and blood pressure. Those with pre-existing heart conditions or a history of heart disease should consult a healthcare professional before using magic mushrooms.

Medication interactions: As previously mentioned, combining magic mushrooms with certain medications, particularly psychiatric medications such as SSRIs, can lead to adverse effects or diminished efficacy. Consult with a healthcare professional familiar with magic mushrooms and your specific medication regimen to ensure safe use.

Allergies: Although rare, some individuals may experience an allergic reaction to magic mushrooms. If you have a known allergy to mushrooms or mold, proceed cautiously and consider discussing your concerns with a healthcare professional.

Emotional challenges: Magic mushroom experiences can be emotionally intense and may bring up unresolved trauma or painful emotions. It is crucial to have a supportive and knowledgeable guide or therapist to help navigate these challenges and ensure a safe and therapeutic experience.

Addiction potential: While magic mushrooms have a low potential for addiction, it is essential to approach their use responsibly and not rely on them as the sole solution for PTSD or personal growth. It is recommended to use them as part of a holistic healing plan that includes other therapies and lifestyle changes.

It is always essential to prioritize safety and well-being when using magic mushrooms for PTSD treatment or personal growth. Consult with a knowledgeable healthcare professional or therapist to discuss any potential risks or contraindications relevant to your unique situation and make informed decisions about incorporating magic mushrooms into your healing journey.

Resources and Further Exploration

Embarking on a healing journey with magic mushrooms can be exciting and challenging. To support you in this process, we have compiled a list of resources and avenues for further exploration. This chapter offers an overview of books, research articles, organizations, and online platforms that can deepen your understanding of the therapeutic use of magic mushrooms for PTSD and personal growth. By engaging with these resources, you can build a strong foundation of knowledge and connect with others who share your passion for healing and self-discovery.

In the following sections, we will introduce you to various resources, including:

A. Books on psychedelics, PTSD, and personal growth
B. Research articles and scientific publications
C. Non-profit organizations and advocacy groups
D. Online forums and communities
E. Podcasts and multimedia resources
F. Workshops, retreats, and professional training

By exploring these resources, you will gain valuable insights and perspectives on the world of magic mushrooms and their potential for transformative healing. This will enhance your journey and contribute to these powerful therapeutic tools' broader understanding and acceptance.

Books on Psychedelics, PTSD, and Personal Growth

The following books offer a wealth of information on the therapeutic use of psychedelics, the nature of PTSD, and practices for personal growth. These resources can provide a solid foundation for understanding the healing potential of magic mushrooms and help you navigate your journey toward recovery and self-discovery.

1. "Microdosing Magic" by True Eira
2. "The Psychedelic Explorer's Guide" by James Fadiman
3. "How to Change Your Mind" by Michael Pollan
4. "The Body Keeps the Score" by Bessel van der Kolk
5. "Waking the Tiger: Healing Trauma" by Peter A. Levine
6. "PTSD: From Surviving to Thriving" by Pete Walker
7. "Radical Acceptance" by Tara Brach
8. "The Untethered Soul" by Michael A. Singer
9. "A Really Good Day" by Ayelet Waldman
10. "Psychedelic Psychotherapy" by R. Coleman
11. "DMT: The Spirit Molecule" by Rick Strassman

These books cover a range of topics, from the science and history of psychedelics to the intricacies of trauma and personal growth. By exploring these resources, you can deepen your understanding of the healing potential of magic mushrooms and how they can support your journey towards recovery from PTSD.

Research Articles and Scientific Publications

Numerous scientific publications and research articles have explored the therapeutic potential of magic mushrooms and their use in treating PTSD and other mental health disorders. Here is a list of some notable studies and reviews that can help you stay informed about the latest research in the field:

1. Carhart-Harris, R. L., et al. (2016). Psilocybin with psychological support for treatment-resistant depression: an open-label feasibility study. The Lancet Psychiatry, 3(7), 619-627.
2. Griffiths, R. R., et al. (2016). Psilocybin produces substantial and sustained decreases in depression and anxiety in patients with life-threatening cancer: A

randomized double-blind trial. Journal of Psychopharmacology, 30(12), 1181-1197.

3. Johnson, M. W., et al. (2014). Pilot study of the 5-HT2AR agonist psilocybin in the treatment of tobacco addiction. Journal of Psychopharmacology, 28(11), 983-992.

4. Mithoefer, M. C., et al. (2019). MDMA-assisted psychotherapy for treatment of PTSD: study design and rationale for phase 3 trials based on pooled analysis of six phase 2 randomized controlled trials. Psychopharmacology, 236(9), 2735-2745.

5. Ross, S., et al. (2016). Rapid and sustained symptom reduction following psilocybin treatment for anxiety and depression in patients with life-threatening cancer: A randomized controlled trial. Journal of Psychopharmacology, 30(12), 1165-1180.

These research articles and scientific publications offer a glimpse into the growing body of evidence supporting the use of magic mushrooms and other psychedelics in treating PTSD and other mental health disorders. By staying up-to-date with the latest research, you can make informed decisions about your own healing journey and better understand the potential benefits and risks associated with magic mushroom therapy.

Non-profit Organizations and Advocacy Groups

Many non-profit organizations and advocacy groups are dedicated to researching, educating, and supporting psychedelic therapies, including magic mushrooms. These organizations often provide valuable resources and information to help individuals navigate the world of psychedelic healing. Here is a list of some prominent non-profit organizations and advocacy groups in this field:

1. Multidisciplinary Association for Psychedelic Studies (MAPS): MAPS is a leading non-profit organization that

promotes and supports scientific research and education about the benefits of psychedelic substances, including magic mushrooms, in treating mental health disorders. Their website (maps.org) offers a wealth of information, including research publications, clinical trial updates, and educational materials.

2. Beckley Foundation: The Beckley Foundation is a UK-based organization that conducts research into psychedelic substances and advocates for evidence-based drug policy reform. Their website (beckleyfoundation.org) provides information on their research projects, policy initiatives, and educational resources.

3. The Third Wave: The Third Wave is an online platform that provides reliable information on psychedelic substances, including magic mushrooms, and promotes their responsible use. They offer resources such as microdosing guides, research articles, and educational content. Visit their website at thethirdwave.co.

4. Psychedelic Science: Psychedelic Science is an organization that brings together the international psychedelic research community to share knowledge and collaborate on research projects. They host conferences and events, and their website (psychedelicscience.org) features a library of research articles, videos, and presentations.

5. The Psychedelic Society: This UK-based organization promotes the responsible use of psychedelic substances for personal growth and therapeutic purposes. They offer educational events, workshops, and online resources. Visit their website at psychedelicsociety.org.uk.

These non-profit organizations and advocacy groups are crucial in advancing our understanding of the therapeutic potential of magic mushrooms and other psychedelics. By engaging with these organizations and supporting their work, you can contribute to the growth of this field and help make these powerful tools more accessible to those in need.

Online Forums and Communities

Connecting with others who share an interest in magic mushrooms and psychedelic therapy can be a valuable source of support, information, and inspiration. There are various online forums and communities where you can ask questions, share experiences, and learn from others who are exploring the use of psychedelics for healing and personal growth. Here are some popular online forums and communities to consider joining:

1. Shroomery (shroomery.org): Shroomery is a comprehensive online forum dedicated to magic mushrooms, providing a wealth of information on cultivation, identification, experiences, and more. The forum also has sections on psychedelic therapy, microdosing, and general discussions related to the use of magic mushrooms.
2. Reddit (reddit.com): Reddit is a vast online platform with numerous subreddits dedicated to psychedelics and their therapeutic uses. Some notable subreddits include r/psychedelics, r/shrooms, and r/microdosing. These subreddits provide a space for users to share experiences, ask questions, and discuss the latest research and news related to magic mushrooms and other psychedelics.
3. The DMT Nexus (dmt-nexus.me): Although primarily focused on DMT, The DMT Nexus is a well-established forum that also discusses other psychedelics, including magic mushrooms. The forum covers a wide range of topics, including experiences, research, cultivation, and harm reduction.
4. The Third Wave Community (community.thethirdwave.co): The Third Wave, an organization dedicated to promoting the responsible use

of psychedelics, has an online community where members can discuss their experiences, ask questions, and share resources related to psychedelics, including magic mushrooms.

5. Erowid (erowid.org): Erowid is an online library and resource center that provides information about psychoactive plants and chemicals. While it is not a traditional forum, the site has an extensive collection of user-submitted experience reports, which can be an invaluable source of insight and knowledge.

These online forums and communities can offer valuable support and information to those interested in exploring the healing potential of magic mushrooms. Remember always to be respectful, open-minded, and considerate when engaging with others in these spaces, and keep in mind that individual experiences and perspectives can vary widely.

Podcasts and Multimedia Resources

Podcasts and multimedia resources are excellent ways to learn more about magic mushrooms, psychedelic therapy, and personal growth. By exploring these resources, you can deepen your understanding of the subject matter, hear inspiring stories and interviews, and stay up-to-date with the latest research and developments in the field. Here are some popular podcasts and multimedia resources related to psychedelics and healing:

1. The Psychedelic Experience (psychedelicexperience.net/podcast): This podcast covers a wide range of topics related to psychedelics, including personal stories, interviews with experts, and discussions on various therapeutic approaches. It aims to promote responsible and informed use of psychedelics for healing and personal growth.

2. The Third Wave Podcast (thethirdwave.co/podcast): The Third Wave Podcast, hosted by Paul Austin, features interviews with experts in the field of psychedelic research, therapy, and culture. Episodes explore various aspects of psychedelics, including their potential for treating mental health disorders, personal transformation, and societal change.

3. The Psychedelic Therapy Podcast (maps.org/podcast): Produced by the Multidisciplinary Association for Psychedelic Studies (MAPS), this podcast features interviews with researchers, therapists, and advocates working on the forefront of psychedelic therapy. The podcast covers topics such as clinical trials, cultural perspectives, and the future of psychedelic medicine.

4. The Tim Ferriss Show (tim.blog/podcast): While not exclusively focused on psychedelics, The Tim Ferriss Show has featured several episodes with prominent figures in the field, such as Michael Pollan, Roland Griffiths, and Rick Doblin. These episodes provide valuable insights into the history, science, and potential therapeutic applications of psychedelics like magic mushrooms.

5. Psychedelic Science (psychedelicscience.org/videos): Psychedelic Science is a website that shares video presentations from past conferences organized by MAPS and other organizations. The site hosts a vast collection of lectures and panel discussions featuring leading researchers and experts in the field of psychedelic medicine.

By exploring these podcasts and multimedia resources, you can deepen your understanding of magic mushrooms, their therapeutic potential, and the broader context of psychedelic research and therapy. These resources provide valuable insights and perspectives that can help inform your personal journey and contribute to a more well-rounded understanding of the healing potential of psychedelics.

Workshops, Retreats, and Professional Training

For those interested in deepening their understanding of magic mushrooms and psychedelic therapy, attending workshops, retreats, and professional training programs can be a valuable investment. These events and programs can provide practical knowledge, hands-on experience, and the opportunity to connect with like-minded individuals. Here are some options to consider:

1. Psychedelic Science conferences (maps.org/conference): The Multidisciplinary Association for Psychedelic Studies (MAPS) hosts international conferences that bring together researchers, clinicians, and advocates to share the latest findings in psychedelic science. These events often include workshops, panel discussions, and networking opportunities.

2. Psychedelic Integration workshops (being-true-to-you.com): Being True to You offers online and in-person workshops on psychedelic integration, harm reduction, and personal growth. Their programs aim to provide practical tools and strategies for those seeking to incorporate psychedelics into their healing and personal development journey.

3. Psychedelic retreats (synthesisretreat.com, mycomeditations.com): Psychedelic retreat centers like Synthesis and MycoMeditations provide legal, professionally guided magic mushroom experiences in countries where psilocybin is not prohibited. These retreats often include group therapy, workshops, and other supportive activities to help participants maximize the benefits of their psychedelic experiences.

4. Professional training programs (ciis.edu/academics/graduate-programs/psychedelic-therapies-and-research, maps.org/training): Several organizations, such as the California Institute of Integral Studies (CIIS) and MAPS, offer professional training programs for therapists and other mental health professionals interested in incorporating psychedelic therapy into their practices. These programs cover the therapeutic use of psychedelics, harm reduction strategies, and ethical considerations.

5. Holotropic Breathwork workshops (holotropic.com): Holotropic Breathwork, developed by Dr. Stanislav Grof, is a powerful non-pharmacological technique that can induce altered states of consciousness similar to those experienced during psychedelic therapy. Attending workshops or trainings in Holotropic Breathwork can provide valuable insights into the healing potential of non-ordinary states of consciousness and complement the use of magic mushrooms in PTSD treatment.

By participating in workshops, retreats, and professional training programs, you can further your understanding of magic mushrooms, their therapeutic applications, and the broader context of psychedelic healing. These experiences can help you integrate the insights gained from magic mushrooms into your own healing journey or support others on their path to recovery.

References

1. Carhart-Harris, R. L., Roseman, L., Bolstridge, M., Demetriou, L., Pannekoek, J. N., Wall, M. B., ... & Leech, R. (2017). Psilocybin for treatment-resistant depression: fMRI-measured brain mechanisms. Scientific Reports, 7(1), 1-11. https://doi.org/10.1038/s41598-017-13282-7

2. Carhart-Harris, R. L., Bolstridge, M., Rucker, J., Day, C. M., Erritzoe, D., Kaelen, M., ... & Nutt, D. J. (2016). Psilocybin with psychological support for treatment-resistant depression: An open-label feasibility study. The Lancet Psychiatry, 3(7), 619-627. https://doi.org/10.1016/S2215-0366(16)30065-7

3. Davis, A. K., Barrett, F. S., & Griffiths, R. R. (2020). Psychological flexibility mediates the relationship between acute psychedelic effects and subjective decreases in depression and anxiety. Journal of Contextual Behavioral Science, 15, 39-45. https://doi.org/10.1016/j.jcbs.2019.11.004

4. Fadiman, J. (2011). The psychedelic explorer's guide: Safe, therapeutic, and sacred journeys. Simon and Schuster.

5. Gasser, P., Kirchner, K., & Passie, T. (2015). LSD-assisted psychotherapy for anxiety associated with a life-threatening disease: A qualitative study of acute and sustained subjective effects. Journal of Psychopharmacology, 29(1), 57-68. https://doi.org/10.1177/0269881114555249

6. Griffiths, R. R., Johnson, M. W., Carducci, M. A., Umbricht, A., Richards, W. A., Richards, B. D., ... & Klinedinst, M. A. (2016). Psilocybin produces substantial and sustained decreases in depression and anxiety in patients with life-threatening cancer: A randomized double-blind trial. Journal of Psychopharmacology, 30(12), 1181-1197. https://doi.org/10.1177/0269881116675513

7. Johnson, M. W., Garcia-Romeu, A., Cosimano, M. P., & Griffiths, R. R. (2014). Pilot study of the 5-HT2AR agonist psilocybin in the treatment of tobacco addiction. Journal of Psychopharmacology, 28(11), 983-992. https://doi.org/10.1177/0269881114548296

8. Kelmendi, B., Adams, T. G., Yarnell, S., Southwick, S., Abdallah, C. G., & Krystal, J. H. (2016). PTSD: From neurobiology to pharmacological treatments. European Journal of Psychotraumatology, 7(1), 31858. https://doi.org/10.3402/ejpt.v7.31858

9. MAPS (Multidisciplinary Association for Psychedelic Studies). (n.d.). Retrieved from https://www.maps.org/

10. Mithoefer, M. C., Mithoefer, A. T., Feduccia, A. A., Jerome, L., Wagner, M., Wymer, J., ... & Yazar-Klosinski, B. (2018). 3,4-methylenedioxymethamphetamine (MDMA)-assisted psychotherapy for post-traumatic stress disorder in military veterans, firefighters, and police officers: A randomised, double-blind, dose-response, phase 2 clinical trial. The Lancet Psychiatry, 5(6), 486-497. https://doi.org/10.1016/S2215-0366(18)30135-4

11. Nichols, D. E. (2016). Psychedelics. Pharmacological Reviews, 68(2), 264-355. https://doi.org/10.1124/pr.115.011478

12. Nutt, D. J., & Carhart-Harris, R. L. (2021). The current status of psychedelics in psychiatry. JAMA Psychiatry, 78(2), 121-122. https://doi.org/10.1001/jamapsychiatry.2020.2176

13. Pollan, M. (2018). How to change your mind: What the new science of psychedelics teaches us about consciousness, dying, addiction, depression, and transcendence. Penguin.

14. Reiche, S., Hermle, L., Gutwinski, S., Jungaberle, H., Gasser, P., & Majić, T. (2017). Serotonergic hallucinogens in the treatment of anxiety and depression in patients suffering from a life-threatening disease: A systematic

review. Progress in Neuro-Psychopharmacology and Biological Psychiatry, 81, 1-10. https://doi.org/10.1016/j.pnpbp.2017.09.012

15. Ross, S., Bossis, A., Guss, J., Agin-Liebes, G., Malone, T., Cohen, B., ... & Su, Z. (2016). Rapid and sustained symptom reduction following psilocybin treatment for anxiety and depression in patients with life-threatening cancer: A randomized controlled trial. Journal of Psychopharmacology, 30(12), 1165-1180. https://doi.org/10.1177/0269881116675512

16. Stamets, P. (2018). Psilocybin mushrooms of the world: An identification guide. Ten Speed Press.

17. Swanson, L. R. (2018). Unifying theories of psychedelic drug effects. Frontiers in Pharmacology, 9, 172. https://doi.org/10.3389/fphar.2018.00172

18. Vollenweider, F. X., & Kometer, M. (2010). The neurobiology of psychedelic drugs: Implications for the treatment of mood disorders. Nature Reviews Neuroscience, 11(9), 642-651. https://doi.org/10.1038/nrn2884

19. Zeifman, R. J., & Palhano-Fontes, F. (2021). The efficacy, tolerability, and safety of serotonergic psychedelics for the management of mood, anxiety, and substance-use

THANKS FOR READING

Thank you for reading this book! We hope it has enriched your understanding of entheogens and their role in self-discovery, healing, and personal growth.

To continue your journey and further connect with the True Eira community, we invite you to claim your exclusive gift at trueeira.com/free, which supports your entheogen exploration.

As you delve deeper into this transformative path, please leave a review to share your thoughts and experiences. Your feedback not only helps others in their journey but also contributes to the growth of our community.

We appreciate your engagement with the True Eira community and look forward to supporting you on your path to wholeness and well-being as we collectively explore self-discovery, healing, and personal growth.

Visit

trueeira.com/test

Find Your Microdose Personality

TRUE
EIRA

OUR MISSION

At True Eira, our mission is to empower individuals in their journey toward self-discovery, healing, and personal growth by offering comprehensive resources that blend ancient wisdom with modern practices. We strive to cultivate a compassionate, knowledgeable, and responsible community of explorers united in the pursuit of genuine transformation. By respecting time-honored traditions and integrating cutting-edge scientific advancements, our goal is to create a supportive space that contributes to both individual upliftment and the liberation and flourishing of humankind.

TRUE EIRA ORIGINS

True Eira was conceived from Travis Eric's life-altering experiences, where he recognized the transformative potential of entheogens for both personal growth and healing. Fueled by a deep-seated desire to empower others, Travis has committed himself to disseminating invaluable insights about attaining wholeness, navigating universal laws, and unleashing untapped human potential. Understanding the complexities of modern life, he found it essential to integrate the enduring wisdom of the past, creating a holistic approach to well-being.

This vision materialized into True Eira, which has blossomed into a nurturing hub for individuals devoted to self-exploration and transformation. At its core, the platform encapsulates Travis's mission to guide others in unveiling their intrinsic power in a balanced and harmonious manner. Here, ancient wisdom meets contemporary challenges, providing a robust set of tools and a supportive community, all aligned in unlocking the full spectrum of human potential.

TRUE
EIRA

THE ESSENCE OF TRUE EIRA

The name "True Eira" holds deep significance, inspired by Eir (or Eira), the Norse goddess of healing. In Norse mythology, Eira is known for her wisdom and expertise in healing and medicine, often associated with physical and spiritual well-being. By invoking the essence of Eira, we aim to embody her healing spirit and create a space that facilitates growth, self-discovery, and personal transformation.

The term "True" in our name signifies our commitment to authenticity and integrity in exploring the vast potential of human growth and self-discovery. We strive to provide reliable, research-based information and resources while honoring the ancient traditions that have long recognized the healing powers of various practices, including using entheogens.

Combining Eira's healing essence with our dedication to authenticity, the name "True Eira" represents our mission to empower individuals on their journey towards self-discovery, healing, and personal growth through a holistic approach, encompassing ancient and modern wisdom practices.

TRUE
EIRA